Inside Rea

THE ACADEMIC WORD LIST IN CONTEXT

By Kent Richmond

Series Director: Cheryl Boyd Zimmerman

4

OXFORD
UNIVERSITY PRESS

OXFORD
UNIVERSITY PRESS

198 Madison Avenue
New York, NY 10016 USA

Great Clarendon Street, Oxford OX2 6DP UK

Oxford University Press is a department of the University of Oxford.
It furthers the University's objective of excellence in research, scholarship,
and education by publishing worldwide in

Oxford New York

Auckland Cape Town Dar es Salaam Hong Kong Karachi
Kuala Lumpur Madrid Melbourne Mexico City Nairobi
New Delhi Shanghai Taipei Toronto

With offices in

Argentina Austria Brazil Chile Czech Republic France Greece
Guatemala Hungary Italy Japan Poland Portugal Singapore
South Korea Switzerland Thailand Turkey Ukraine Vietnam

OXFORD and OXFORD ENGLISH are registered trademarks of
Oxford University Press.

© Oxford University Press 2009

Database right Oxford University Press (maker)

Library of Congress Cataloging-in-Publication Data

Burgmeier, Arline

Inside reading 1: the academic word list in context / Arline Burgmeier.

p. cm.

ISBN 978-0-19-441612-2 (pbk. w/ cdrom)

1. English language—Textbooks for foreign speakers. 2. Vocabulary. I. Title.

PE1128.B846 2007

428.2'4—dc22   2007023406

Senior Managing Editor: Patricia O'Neill
Editor: Dena Daniel
Design Manager: Maj-Britt Hagsted
Production Artist: Julie Armstrong
Compositor: TSI Graphics Inc.
Cover design: Stacy Merlin
Manufacturing Manager: Shanta Persaud
Manufacturing Controller: Zai Jawat Ali

Student book pack ISBN: 978 0 19 441615 3

Student book ISBN: 978 0 19 441609 2

Printed in Hong Kong

10 9 8 7 6 5 4 3 2

ACKNOWLEDGMENTS

Cover art: PunchStock: Elephant; Zefa / Corbis: Estelle Klawitter: Guitar

The publisher would like to thank TSI Graphics and the author for the illustrations used in this book.

The publisher would like to thank the following for their permission to reproduce photographs: Bruce Dale/National Geographic Image Collection: 3; Gerry Pearce/Alamy: 4; Frances Roberts / Alamy: 10; Leonard McCombe/Time & Life Pictures/Getty Images: 24; Courtesy of Columbia Pictures: 40; Jennifer Weinberg / Alamy: 88; Kim Kulish/Corbis: 115; M. Bonani and F. Mondada, Ecole Polytechnique Fédérale de Lausanne: 131; © Robert Harding Picture Library Ltd / Alamy: 147

The publisher would like to acknowledge these valuable sources of information incorporated into the articles and activities of this textbook: **Unit 1**, "Animal Olympics," National Wildlife Federation, 2005, www.eNature.com; "Born to Run," by Ingfei Chen, *Discover* (Vol. 27, No. 5, May 2006); "Born to Run," by Adam Summers, *Natural History* (Vol. 144, Issue 3, April 2005); "Faster than a Hyena? Running May Make Humans Special," by Carl Zimmer, *Science* (Vol. 306, Issue 5700, Nov. 19, 2004). **Unit 2**, "Cell Phones, Driving Don't Mix," Science Daily (www.sciencedaily.com, posted Dec. 9, 2005); "Executive Control of Cognitive Processes in Task Switching" by Joshua S. Rubinstein, Daved E. Meyer, and Jeffrey E. Evans, *Journal of Experimental Psychology* (Vol. 27, No. 4, 2001); "The Limits of Multitasking," by Klaus Manhart, *Scientific American Mind* (Dec. 2004); "You're Getting Very Sleepy," © 2004 by the American Psychological Association. Adapted with permission. **Unit 3**, "Aroma-Rama and Smell-O-Vision." www.filmsite.org; "Hollywood Ballyhoo," Belknap Collection for the Performing Arts, University of Florida; *Leonard Maltin's 2007 Movie Guide, 2006*, New York, Plume; "William Castle," Internet Movie Database (www.imdb.com); "Ray Harryhausen," by Bruce Elder, *All Movie Guide*; "Ray Harryhausen," Internet Movie Database; "Ray Harryhausen Biography," 2006, the Official Website of Ray Harryhausen (www.rayharryhausen.com); *The Fantastic Films of Ray Harryhausen: Legendary Monster Series*, Sony Pictures DVD, 2004 (liner notes and interview with Ray Harryhausen). **Unit 4**, *"Why Does Music Move Us? Science gets closer to the intersection of biology and creativity,"* by Douglas McLennan, *Wall Street Journal*, Dec. 3, 2005, © 2005 by Dow Jones & Company Inc., adapted with permission; *The Guitar Handbook*, by Ralph Denyer, New York, Alfred A. Knopf, 2002; *Martin & Co., Est. 1833: A History*, by Mike Longworth, Minisink Hills, PA, 4 Maples Press, Inc., 1988; *Clapton's Guitar: Watching Wayne Henderson Build the Perfect Instrument*, by Allen St. John, New York Free Press, 2005; "The Dobro Story," Gibson Guitar web site (www.gibson.com). **Unit 5**, "Device Records Smell to Play Back Later," by Paul Marks, *New Scientist*, (issue 2558, June 29, 2006); "I Smell, Therefore I Think: Did odors give rise to the first words?" by Jaron Lanier, *Discover* (Vol. 27, No. 5, May 2006); *Handbook of Machine Olfaction: Electronic Nose Technology*, T. C. Pearce, S. S. Schiffman, H. T. Nagle, J. W. Gardner (eds), Weinheim, Wiley-VCH, 2002; "Odor Parameters," St. Croix Sensory, 2002 (www.fivesenses.com/Research_OdorParameters.cfm); *This Is Your Brain on Music: The Science of a Human Obsession*, by Daniel J. Levitin, New York, Dutton, 2006; *The Enjoyment of Music: An Introduction to Perceptive Listening*, by Joseph Machlis and Kristine Forney, 8th Ed., New York, W.W. Norton and Company, Inc., 1999; **Unit 6**, "Bubble bursts on Beanie Babies" by Thomas S. Mulligan, *The Seattle Times*, Aug. 31, 2004; Graph of silver prices, Kitco bullion dealers (www.kitco.com); "When the Tulip Bubble Burst" (book review), by Mike Frankel, *Business Week Online*, April 24, 2000; "Bulb, Bubble, Trouble: That Dutch Tulip Bubble Wasn't So Crazy After All," by Daniel Gross, *Slate* (posted July 16, 2004); *Extraordinary Popular Delusions and the Madness of Crowds*, by Charles MacKay, LL.D., New York, Harmony Books, 1980 (originally published 1841); "Flower Power: The Lessons" (book review), by Kim Phillips-Fein, *The Nation*, June 26, 2000; UCLA Department of Economics, Earl A. Thompson and Jonathan Treussard (Levine's Working Paper Archive, April 30, 2003). **Unit 7**, Excerpt from *Blink*, by Malcolm Gladwell, © 2005 by Malcolm Gladwell. By permission of Little, Brown & Company. *The Wisdom of Crowds*, by James Surowiecki, New York, Anchor Books, 2004, 2005. **Unit 8**, *The Google Story*, by David Vise and Mark Malseed, New York, Delta, 2006; Google's corporate history, Google web site (www.google.com/corporate/history/); Yahoo Finance (http://finance.yahoo.com/). **Unit 9**, "The Swarmbots Are Coming: Ant algorithms get down to business," by Marco Dorigo, *Wired*, Feb. 2004. Adapted and used with permission; "Bye Swarmbots, Hello Swarmanoids," by Emmet Cole, *Wired News*, Nov. 28, 2006. Adapted and used with permission; "The Future of Robotics," by Ray Kurzweil, originally printed in *Popular Science* (Vol. 269, Issue 3, Sep. 2006). Used by permission. **Unit 10**, "Easter' s End," by Jared Diamond, *Discover* (Vol. 16, No. 8, Aug. 1995). Used by permission of the author; Excerpt from "A Monumental Collapse?" by Emma Young, *New Scientist* (Vol. 191 Issue 2562, July 29, 2006). Adapted and used with permission.

Acknowledgments

From the Series Director

Inside Reading represents collaboration as it should be. That is, the project resulted from a balance of expertise from a team at Oxford University Press (OUP) and a collection of skilled participants from several universities. The project would not have happened without considerable investment and talent from both sides.

This idea took root and developed with the collaboration and support of the OUP editorial team. I am particularly grateful to Pietro Alongi, whose vision for this series began with his recognition of the reciprocal relationship between reading and vocabulary. I am also grateful to Dena Daniel, the lead editor on the project, and Janet Aitchison for her involvement in the early stages of this venture.

OUP was joined by the contributions of participants from various academic settings. First, Averil Coxhead, Massey University, New Zealand, created the Academic Word List, a principled, research-based collection of academic words which has led both to much of the research which supports this project and to the materials themselves. Dr. Tom Klammer, Dean of Humanities and Social Sciences at California State University, Fullerton (CSUF), made my participation in this project possible, first by endorsing its value, then by providing the time I needed. Assistance and insight were provided by CSUF participants Patricia Balderas, Arline Burgmeier, and Margaret Plenert, as well as by many TESOL Masters students at CSUF.

Finally, thank you to the many reviewers who gave us feedback along the way: Nancy Baum, **University of Texas at Arlington;** Adele Camus, **George Mason University;** Carole Collins, **Northampton Community College;** Jennifer Farnell, **University of Connecticut**, ALP; Laurie Frazier, **University of Minnesota;** Debbie Gold, **California State University**, Long Beach, ALI; Janet Harclerode and Toni Randall, **Santa Monica Community College;** Marianne Hsu Santelli, **Middlesex County College;** Steve Jones, **Community College of Philadelphia;** Lucille King, **University of Connecticut;** Shalle Leeming, **Academy of Art University**, San Francisco; Gerry Luton, **University of Victoria;** David Mindock, **University of Denver;** and William Morrill, **University of Washington**. This is collaboration indeed!

From the Author

I would like to thank Cheryl Zimmerman as well as Pietro Alongi, Dena Daniel, and the editorial team at Oxford University Press for imagining this project, inviting me to participate, and offering encouragement and expertise. I would like to thank the many program directors I have worked for over the last thirty years, particularly Karen Fox, Arline Burgmeier, and Steve and Tere Ross, who always gave me free rein to try out ideas that lead to projects such as this one. Most of all, I am grateful to my wife, Lynne Richmond, director of the American Language Institute at California State University, Long Beach. She convinced me to take on this project and provided both optimism and advice when I needed it most.

Contents

To the Teacher

There is a natural relationship between academic reading and word learning. *Inside Reading* is a four-level reading and vocabulary series designed to use this relationship to best advantage. Through principled instruction and practice with reading strategies and skills, students will increase their ability to comprehend reading material. Likewise, through a principled approach to the complex nature of vocabulary knowledge, learners will better understand how to make sense of the complex nature of academic word learning. *Inside Reading 4* is intended for students at the advanced level.

Academic Reading and Vocabulary: A Reciprocal Relationship

In the beginning stages of language learning, when the learner is making simple connections between familiar oral words and written forms, vocabulary knowledge plays a crucial role. In later stages, such as those addressed by *Inside Reading*, word learning and reading are increasingly interdependent: rich word knowledge facilitates reading, and effective reading skills facilitate vocabulary comprehension and learning.[1]

The word knowledge that is needed by the reader in this reciprocal process is more than knowledge of definitions.[2] Truly knowing a word well enough to use it in reading (as well as in production) means knowing something about its grammar, word forms, collocations, register, associations, and a great deal about its meaning, including its connotations and multiple meanings.[3] Any of this information may be called upon to help the reader make the inferences needed to understand the word's meaning in a particular text. For example, a passage's meaning can be controlled completely by a connotation

She was *frugal*.   (positive connotation)
She was *stingy*.   (negative connotation)
by grammatical form
He valued his *memory*.
He valued his *memories*.

or an alternate meaning
The *labor* was intense.   (physical work vs. childbirth)

Inside Reading recognizes the complexity of knowing a word. Students are given frequent and varied practice with all aspects of word knowledge. Vocabulary activities are closely related in topic to the reading selections, providing multiple exposures to a word in actual use and opportunities to work with its meanings, grammatical features, word forms, collocations, register, and associations.

To join principled vocabulary instruction with academic reading instruction is both natural and effective. *Inside Reading* is designed to address the reciprocal relationship between reading and vocabulary and to use it to help students develop academic proficiency.

A Closer Look at Academic Reading

Students preparing for academic work benefit from instruction that includes attention to the language as well as attention to the process of reading. The Interactive Reading model indicates that reading is an active process in which readers draw upon *top-down processing* (bringing meaning to the text), as well as *bottom-up processing* (decoding words and other details of language).[4]

The *top-down* aspect of this construct suggests that reading is facilitated by interesting and relevant reading materials that activate a range of knowledge in a reader's mind, knowledge that is refined and extended during the act of reading.

The *bottom-up* aspect of this model suggests that the learner needs to pay attention to language proficiency, including vocabulary. An academic reading course must address the teaching of higher-level reading strategies without neglecting the need for language support.[5]

---

[1] Koda, 2005

[2] See the meta-analysis of L1 vocabulary studies by Stahl & Fairbanks, 1986.

[3] Nation, 1990

[4] Carrell, Devine, and Eskey, 1988

[5] Birch, 2002; Eskey, 1988

Inside Reading addresses both sides of the interactive model. High-interest academic readings and activities provide students with opportunities to draw upon life experience in their mastery of a wide variety of strategies and skills, including

- previewing
- scanning
- using context clues to clarify meaning
- finding the main idea
- summarizing
- making inferences.

Rich vocabulary instruction and practice that targets vocabulary from the Academic Word List (AWL) provide opportunities for students to improve their language proficiency and their ability to decode and process vocabulary.

A Closer Look at Academic Vocabulary

Academic vocabulary consists of those words which are used broadly in all academic domains, but are not necessarily frequent in other domains. They are words in the academic register that are needed by students who intend to pursue higher education. They are not the technical words used in one academic field or another (e.g., *genetics, fiduciary, proton*), but are found in all academic areas, often in a supportive role (*substitute, function, inhibit*).

The most principled and widely accepted list of academic words to date is The Academic Word List (AWL), compiled by Averil Coxhead in 2000. Its selection was based on a corpus of 3.5 million words of running text from academic materials across four academic disciplines: the humanities, business, law, and the physical and life sciences. The criteria for selection of the 570 word families on the AWL was that the words appear frequently and uniformly across a wide range of academic texts, and that they not appear among the first 2000 most common words of English, as identified by the General Service List.[6]

Across the four levels of *Inside Reading*, students are introduced to the 570 word families of the AWL

at a gradual pace of about 15 words per unit. Their usage is authentic, the readings in which they appear are high interest, and the words are practiced and recycled in a variety of activities, facilitating both reading comprehension and word learning.

There has been a great deal of research into the optimal classroom conditions for facilitating word learning. This research points to several key factors.

Noticing: Before new words can be learned, they must be noticed. Schmidt, in his well-known *noticing hypothesis,* states

> noticing is the necessary and sufficient condition for converting input into intake. Incidental learning, on the other hand, is clearly both possible and effective when the demands of a task focus attention on what is to be learned.[7]

Inside Reading facilitates noticing in two ways. Target words are printed in boldface type at their first occurrence to draw the students' attention to their context, usage, and word form. Students are then offered repeated opportunities to focus on them in activities and discussions. *Inside Reading* also devotes activities and tasks to particular target words. This is often accompanied by a presentation box giving information about the word, its family members, and its usage.

Teachers can further facilitate noticing by pre-teaching selected words through "rich instruction," meaning instruction that focuses on what it means to know a word, looks at the word in more than one setting, and involves learners in actively processing the word.[8] *Inside Reading* facilitates rich instruction by providing engaging activities that use and spotlight target words in both written and oral practice.

Repetition: Word learning is incremental. A learner is able to pick up new knowledge about a word with each encounter. Repetition also assists learner memory—multiple exposures at varying intervals dramatically enhance retention.

Repetition alone doesn't account for learning; the types and intervals of repetitions are also important.

---

6 West, 1953; Coxhead 2000
7 Schmidt, 1990, p. 129
8 Nation, 2001, p. 157

Research shows that words are best retained when the practice with a new word is brief but the word is repeated several times at increasing intervals.[9] *Inside Reading* provides multiple exposures to words at varying intervals and recycles vocabulary throughout the book to assist this process.

Learner involvement: Word learning activities are not guaranteed to be effective simply by virtue of being interactive or communicative. Activities or tasks are most effective when learners are most *involved* in them. Optimal involvement is characterized by a learner's own perceived need for the unknown word, the desire to search for the necessary information needed for the task, and the effort expended to compare the word to other words. It has been found that the greater the level of learner involvement, the better the retention.[10]

The activities in *Inside Reading* provide opportunities to be involved in the *use* of target words at two levels:

- "Word level," where words are practiced in isolation for the purpose of focusing on such aspects as meaning, derivation, grammatical features, and associations.
- "Sentence level," where learners respond to the readings by writing and paraphrasing sentences.

Because the activities are grounded in the two high-interest readings of each unit, they provide the teacher with frequent opportunities to optimize learner involvement.

Instruction and practice with varying types of word knowledge: To know a word means to know a great deal about the word.[11] The activities in this book include practice with all aspects of word knowledge: form (both oral and written), meaning, multiple meanings, collocations, grammatical features, derivatives, register, and associations.

Helping students become independent word learners: No single course or book can address all of the words a learner will need. Students should leave a class with new skills and strategies for word learning so that they can notice and effectively practice new words as they encounter them. *Inside Reading* includes several features to help guide students to becoming independent word learners. One is a self-assessment activity, which begins and ends each unit. Students evaluate their level of knowledge of each word, ranging from not knowing a word at all, to word recognition, and then to two levels of word use. This exercise demonstrates the incremental nature of word knowledge, and guides learners toward identifying what they know and what they need to know. Students can make better progress if they accurately identify the aspects of word knowledge they need for themselves. Another feature is the use of references and online resources: To further prepare students to be independent word learners, instruction and practice in dictionary use and online resources are provided throughout the book.

The *Inside Reading* Program

Inside Reading offers students and teachers helpful ancillaries:

Student CD-ROM: The CD-ROM in the back of every student book contains additional practice activities for students to work with on their own. The activities are self-correcting and allow students to redo an activity as many times as they wish.

Instructor's pack: The Instructor's pack contains the answer key for the book along with a test generator CD-ROM. The test generator contains one test per student book unit. Each test consists of a reading passage related to the topic of the unit, which features the target vocabulary. This is followed by reading comprehension and vocabulary questions. Teachers can use each unit's test in full or customize it in a variety of ways.

Inside Reading optimizes the reciprocal relationship between reading and vocabulary by drawing upon considerable research and many years of teaching experience. It provides the resources to help students read well and to use that knowledge to develop both a rich academic vocabulary and overall academic language proficiency.

---

[9] Research findings are inconclusive about the number of repetitions that are needed for retention. Estimates range from 6 to 20. See Nation, 2001, for a discussion of repetition and learning.

[10] Laufer & Hulstijn, 2001

[11] Nation, 1990; 2001

References

Birch, B. M. (2002). *English L2 reading: Getting to the bottom.* Mahwah, N. J.: Lawrence Erlbaum Associates.

Carrel, P.L., Devine, J., & Eskey, D.E. (1988). *Interactive approaches to second language reading.* Cambridge: Cambridge University Press.

Coxhead, A. (2000). A new academic word list. *TESOL Quarterly, 34,* 213–238.

Eskey, D.E. (1988). Holding in the bottom. In P.L. Carrel, J. Devine, & D.E. Eskey, *Interactive approaches to second language reading,* pp. 93–100. Cambridge: Cambridge University Press.

Koda, K. (2005). *Insights into second language reading.* Cambridge: Cambridge University Press.

Laufer, B. (1992). Reading in a foreign language: How does L2 lexical knowledge interact with the reader's general academic ability? *Journal of Research in Reading, 15*(2), 95–103.

Laufer, B. (2005). Instructed second language vocabulary learning: The fault in the 'default hypothesis.' In A. Housen & M. Pierrard (Eds.), *Investigations in Instructed Second Language Acquisition,* pp. 286–303. New York: Mouton de Gruyter.

Laufer, B. & Hulstijn, J. (2001). "Incidental vocabulary acquisition in a second language: The construct of task–induced involvement." *Applied Linguistics, 22*(1),1–26.

Nation, I.S.P. (1990). *Teaching and learning vocabulary.* New York: Newbury House.

Nation, I.S.P. (2001). *Learning vocabulary in another language.* Cambridge: Cambridge University Press.

Schmidt, R. (1990). The role of consciousness in second language learning. *Applied Linguistics, 11,* 129–158.

Schmitt, N. (2000). *Vocabulary in language teaching.* Cambridge: Cambridge University Press.

Schmitt, N. & Zimmerman, C.B. (2002). Derivative word forms: What do learners know? *TESOL Quarterly, 36*(2), 145–171.

Stahl, S.A. & Fairbanks, M.M. (1986). The effects of vocabulary instruction: A model-based meta-analysis. *Review of Educational Research, 56*(1), 72–110.

West, M. (1953). *A general service list of English words.* London: Longman, Green.

Welcome to *Inside Reading*

Inside Reading is a four-level series that develops students' abilities to interact with and access academic reading and vocabulary, preparing them for success in the academic classroom.

There are ten units in *Inside Reading.* Each unit features two readings on a high-interest topic from an academic content area, one or more reading skills and strategies, and work with a set of target word families from the **Academic Word List.**

UNIT OPENER

The opening page of each unit introduces the **content area** and **topic**.

Unit
4
Music

THE POWER OF MUSIC

In this unit, you will

- ⊃ read about how the brain responds to music and how guitars are made.
- ⊃ learn about some features of technical description.
- ⊃ increase your understanding of the target academic words for this unit:

confer	fundamental	manipulate	project	theory
diminish	incorporate	physical	refine	transmit
foundation	intrinsic	prime	stress	

The unit's **goals** and **target academic vocabulary** are presented so that students can start to think about their knowledge of the topic and focus on the reading strategies and target word families they will deal with in this unit.

SELF-ASSESSMENT OF TARGET WORDS

Think carefully about how well you know each target word in this unit. Then, write it in the appropriate column in the chart. When you've finished this unit, come back and reassess your knowledge of the target words.

I have never seen the word before.	I have seen the word but am not sure what it means.	I understand the word when I see or hear it in a sentence.	I have tried to use the word, but I am not sure I am using it correctly.	I use the word with confidence in either speaking *or* writing.	I use the word with confidence, both in speaking *and* writing.

Each unit starts with a **self-assessment activity** to heighten student awareness of their own word knowledge. Students will come back to this activity at the end of the unit to re-assess their knowledge and evaluate their progress.

NOTE

Inside Reading is designed so that units can be taught in order or randomly, depending on students' needs.

THE POWER OF MUSIC   49

READING 1

BEFORE YOU READ

Read these questions. Discuss your answers in small groups.

1. All cultures have music, but cultures and individuals disagree on what sounds good. Is there any kind of music that sounds good to most people?
2. What kind of music do you like most? What makes this music interesting to you?
3. Do you think there will someday be a pill that can make people more creative? Would you take it?

- Before each of the two readings in a unit, students discuss questions or do a short activity to **activate knowledge of the specific topic** dealt with in the reading.

MORE WORDS YOU'LL NEED

auditory: related to hearing
circuitry: a system of electrical pathways (such as neural pathways in the brain)
pitch: the highness or lowness of a musical note
quasi-: prefix meaning "seemingly" or "partially" so

READ

This article reports some of the recent findings concerning the connection between emotional reactions to music and biology.

- Readings represent **a variety of genres**: newspapers, magazines, web sites, press releases, encyclopedias, and books.

- Target vocabulary is bold at its first occurrence to aid recognition. **Vocabulary is recycled** and practiced throughout the unit. Target words are also recycled in subsequent units.

Why Does Music Move Us?

Science gets closer to the intersection of biology and creativity

Researchers are only now beginning to unlock the secrets of the brain. It seems like every month some new study or another comes along to explain why we get addicted to nicotine, or how our neural pathways were changed because we studied piano as children, or how meditation alters our brainwave patterns.

Isolating which part of the brain is responsible for moving your big toe is a neat trick. But what about "softer" functions like figuring out how judgment is formed or music is made? "Why Music Moves Us: The Cognitive Neuroscience[1] of Music," a **conference** at the Swedish Medical Center in Seattle in 2005, tried to ask some fundamental questions about how the brain

We know how the ear catches sound and how the sound waves are translated by about 30,000 auditory nerves into electrical and chemical signals that are **transmitted** to the brain. But how is it that the neurons in the brain translate those signals into something we recognize as music? Scans show that the brain is much more actively engaged with music than with speech. But there is no actual **physical** sound in your brain. No notes. No music. Only neurons.

"The idea of pitch is a mental phenomenon," says Robert Zatorre, professor of neuroscience at McGill University in Montreal. Only the way sounds are organized makes them interesting. Brain scans show that different parts of the brain register activity depending on the kind of music played. Dissonance[2], for example, is generally perceived as unpleasant, and it provokes reactions in a different region of the

READING COMPREHENSION

Reading comprehension questions follow each text to check students' understanding and recycle target vocabulary.

READING COMPREHENSION

A. Mark each sentence as *T* (true) or *F* (false) according to the information in Reading 1. Use the dictionary to help you understand new words.

.... 1. Locating the area of the brain that controls toe movement is impossible.
.... 2. Sound waves themselves do not enter the brain.
.... 3. People need to learn how to speak before they can appreciate music.
.... 4. There is evidence that music may help people with brain injuries.
.... 5. We are now able to improve people's creativity and perception of music with brain implants.
.... 6. The reading says that neuroscience will destroy our appreciation of art.
.... 7. The reading implies that artistic success is entirely a product of the physical brain.
.... 8. The secrets behind artistic success may seem less mysterious in the future.

READING STRATEGIES

Strategy presentation and **practice** accompanies each reading.

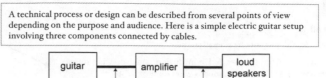

READING STRATEGY: Point of View

A technical process or design can be described from several points of view depending on the purpose and audience. Here is a simple electric guitar setup involving three components connected by cables.

guitar → guitar cable → amplifier → speaker cables → loud speakers

Read these paragraphs describing the diagram above from different points of view. For each paragraph, complete the task.

Description

1. **How do I set it up?**
   Insert one end of a guitar cable into the jack in the electric guitar. Insert the other end of the cable into the input jack on the amplifier. Then run speaker cables from the output jacks of the amplifier to the input terminals of the speakers.

2. **How is it set up or designed?**
   One end of a guitar cable is inserted into the jack in the guitar. The other end is plugged into the input jack in the amplifier. A speaker cable runs from the output jack of the amplifier to the input jack of the loud speaker.

Task

This version gives instructions to the reader. Underline the verbs that tell the reader what to do.

This version describes the setup without indicating who set it up. Underline any intransitive verbs. (See Unit 3, page 45, for more on transitive and intransitive verbs.)

VOCABULARY ACTIVITIES

There are **two types of vocabulary activities** that follow each reading. The first type of activity is **word level and mostly receptive,** focusing on meanings and word family members.

The second type of vocabulary activity is **sentence level and mostly productive.** Each unit features work with collocations. These activities can also include work with register, associations, connotations, and learner dictionaries.

VOCABULARY ACTIVITIES

Noun	Verb	Adjective	Adverb
....	....	intrinsic	intrinsically
manipulation	manipulate	manipulative	manipulatively
projectile* projection	project	projected	....
refinement	refine	refined	....
stress	stress	stressful stressed	stressfully
theory	theorize	theoretical	theoretically

*The noun *project* will be treated in Unit 9.

A. Fill in the blanks with a target word from the chart that completes the sentence in a grammatical and meaningful way. Be sure to use the correct form.

1. Although it is .... possible for a guitar to be made of a single wood, most guitars use a variety of woods.

2. Wood is a popular material for guitars because it can be .... in many ways, including shaping, bowing, and slicing.

3. Woods are selected for their ability to impart sound, their beauty when finished, and their ability to withstand the .... of day-to-day playing.

4. Several approaches are available for .... sound in large spaces.

5. The technology for amplifying acoustic guitars is still being ....

B. In the reading, *stress* refers to physical force, but it can also refer to emphasis or to psychological pressure. In your notebook, write sentences that link these words in a meaningful and grammatical way. Compare sentences with a partner.

1. consultant / stress / need / better quality control
   The consultant stressed the need for better quality control.

2. teacher / stress / read Chapter 5 very carefully

3. assign / too many tasks at once / stressful

4. must / greater stress on / open / new markets for our products

5. psychologist / stress / multitasking / not a reliable strategy for saving time

feel stres........ / go to sche......... he same tim...

NOTE

Each unit ends with topics and projects that teachers can use to take the lesson further. This section includes class discussion topics, online research projects, and essay ideas.

THE STRENGTH TO SURVIVE

In this unit, you will

- ⊃ read about the amazing physical abilities of animals and humans.
- ⊃ practice the reading skills of skimming, scanning, and outlining.
- ⊃ increase your understanding of the target academic words for this unit:

achieve	element	feature	release	undergo
area	exceed	maintain	sole	welfare
duration	facilitate	preliminary	transfer	

SELF-ASSESSMENT OF TARGET WORDS

Learning a word is a gradual process.

- First, you learn to *recognize* the word. This means you know something about its spelling, pronunciation, and meanings.
- Next, you learn to *use* the word. This requires that you understand its spelling, pronunciation, grammar, and much more.

When you truly know a word, you can both recognize it and use it accurately.

Read the target words for this unit in the objectives box above. Think carefully about how well you know each word. Then, write each word in the appropriate column in this chart. When you've finished this unit, come back and reassess your knowledge of the target words.

I have never seen the word before.	I have seen the word but am not sure what it means.	I understand the word when I see or hear it in a sentence.	I have tried to use the word, but I am not sure I am using it correctly.	I use the word with confidence in either speaking *or* writing.	I use the word with confidence, both in speaking *and* writing.

BEFORE YOU READ

Read these questions. Discuss your answers in a small group.

1. Many articles in magazines or newspapers and magazine-style television shows keep our attention by providing interesting trivia. What is trivia? Why do people find trivia so entertaining? Do you like trivia?

2. Speaking of trivia, how are you on animal names? Use the chart below to categorize the animals listed in the box based on your own knowledge. For those you don't know, skim through the reading and find information on them. Then, come back and categorize them in the chart.

cheetah	roadrunner	eel	puffin
gazelle	coyote	wildebeest	thick-billed murre
antelope	swift	zebra	beetle
falcon	albatross	dovekie	
ostrich	salmon	loon	

Bird	Fish	Insect	Grazing Animal	Cat	Canine

MORE WORDS YOU'LL NEED

predator: an animal that kills other animals for food

prey: an animal that a predator kills for food

migrate: (for animals and birds) move from one part of the world to another according to the season

Metric conversions for measurements used in this unit:

1 foot = 0.3 meters	1 pound = 0.45 kilograms
1 yard = 0.9 meters	1 ton = 2,000 pounds (907 kilograms)
1 mile = 1.6 kilometers	

READ

In a sense all animals are Olympians—they have skills at which they excel. This article from the National Wildlife Federation discusses how animals would perform in five categories of Olympic competition—sprinting, long-distance running, diving, jumping, and weightlifting.

Animal Olympics

Athleticism, speed, strength, power, endurance: Humans celebrate these attributes in such events as the Olympic Games. In the animal kingdom, however, these qualities are necessary for the
5 **welfare** and survival of the individual and society. Animals perform amazing feats every day, not with the purpose of winning or being named the best, but in order to eat, seek and catch prey, mate, escape predators, and endure the **elements**.

10 **Sprinting**

The cheetah is said to be the fastest running mammal on earth, with a top sprinting speed of 70 miles per hour (mph). Why does it run so fast? To catch the fleet-footed gazelles and antelopes
15 on which it feeds. In its natural habitat in the grasslands of Africa, the cheetah can outrun its fleetest prey. Like human sprinters, it cannot **maintain** its top speed for long and must take down its prey within a distance of about 300 yards.
20 If the cheetah lived in North America, it might meet its match. The pronghorn antelope has been clocked at close to 70 mph and can run for long distances at 30 to 45 mph. Interestingly enough, these two animals run these top speeds for different
25 reasons: the cheetah runs in pursuit, whereas the pronghorn runs to escape.

The peregrine falcon is widely acknowledged to be the fastest moving bird, **achieving** astonishing speeds when it dives for prey. Some sources cite a
30 top speed of 200 mph, while others put the figure at about 120 mph. Either way, it would be hard for any other bird to escape it. On foot, the fastest bird is the ostrich, which can run about 40 mph. It outpaces the greater roadrunner, North America's
35 fastest running bird, which tops out at about 25 mph. Coyotes, incidentally, can also outrun roadrunners with a cruising speed of 25–30 mph and a top speed of 40 mph.

The greater roadrunner on the move

Marathon

40 The Olympic Marathon, a paltry 26 miles, doesn't come close to the marathons some animals endure. Take the Arctic tern, for instance. It migrates between the North and South Poles, covering a distance of as much as 30,000 miles each
45 and every year. Some birds spend long **durations**, even most of their lives, in flight. Swifts, for example, have very underdeveloped legs and live almost entirely on the wing. Some seabirds, such as the sooty tern, fly for years without landing. The
50 wandering albatross is named for its ability to fly thousands of miles on feeding trips.

Fish can make long-distance migrations as well. Some salmon, swimming between the ocean and

the rivers in which they spawn, cover 2,000 miles.
55 European eels are said to swim up to 3,700 miles to
reach their breeding grounds in the Sargasso Sea
located in the Atlantic Ocean.

The great annual migration of wildebeests
and zebras in the African Serengeti covers about
60 2,000 miles. But the longest annual migration
by a mammal is the 10,000-mile circuit made by
the gray whale from the Arctic to its warm winter
calving areas and back again.

Diving

65 The sperm whale is generally acknowledged to
be the deepest diving mammal, but the northern
bottlenose whale is not far behind. The sperm
whale is known to dive a mile (5,280 feet) or deeper
and to stay under for durations **exceeding** two
70 hours. The bottlenose is said to dive at least 5,000
feet and is also able to remain submerged for two
hours. If the two were competing in an Olympic
event, the odds would be about even.

There is little competition for the deepest diving
75 bird, the emperor penguin, which can dive to a
depth of 1,770 feet. Outside of the penguin family,
the thick-billed murre may be one of the emperor's
nearest competitors; it is thought to dive to
600–700 feet. Dovekies (300 feet), loons (250 feet),
80 Atlantic puffins (160 feet), and long-tailed ducks
(130 feet) are all superb divers but are no match for
the emperor penguin.

Jumping

Some types of kangaroos can leap a distance of
85 30 feet. White-tailed deer, when bounding, can
cover almost the same distance. But the true long-
jump champion is probably the inch-long southern
cricket frog, which makes leaps exceeding 60 times
its body length.

The red kangaroo

90 As for the high jump, the red kangaroo can hurdle
a 10-foot fence. North America's white-tailed deer
can hurdle an obstacle 8 1/2 feet high. Those leapers
have got nothing on the lowly spittlebug though,
which jumps 115 times its body height. The deer
95 and kangaroo would have to jump about 600 feet to
compete with the spittlebug!

Weightlifting

No animal on earth can lift as much weight as
the African elephant, which can pick up a one-
100 ton weight with its trunk. Relative to body size,
however, the elephant doesn't even come close
to the strongest animal on earth. What is it? The
rhinoceros beetle. This rather strange-looking little
creature can transport objects weighing 850 times
105 its own body weight. The elephant, carrying only
one fourth of its body weight, isn't even close in this
contest.

At the Olympic Games, the fastest runners,
highest jumpers, and most skillful divers
110 win medals and worldwide acclaim. In the
animal world, no medals are awarded, and
individuals don't often achieve fame for their
accomplishments. Rather, the amazing athletic
feats performed by animals enable them to
115 escape danger, catch food, impress a mate, and
live another day.

READING COMPREHENSION

Mark each sentence as *T* (true) or *F* (false) according to the information in Reading 1. Use the dictionary to help you understand new words.

.... **1.** Pronghorn antelopes are the cheetah's prey.

.... **2.** A sperm whale can hold its breath for a duration of two hours.

.... **3.** Peregrine falcons eat other birds.

.... **4.** A cheetah can run a mile in less than a minute.

.... **5.** Coyotes can run a mile in under 2 minutes.

.... **6.** No animal can dive deeper than the emperor penguin.

.... **7.** The southern cricket frog makes leaps exceeding 100 times its body length.

.... **8.** Relative to body weight, a healthy human being can lift more than an elephant.

READING STRATEGY: Skimming and Scanning

How fast should you read? Here are typical words-per-minute ranges for each type of reading:

Purpose	Speed
for memorization	very slow: under 100 words per minute
for learning	slow: 100–200 words per minute
for comprehension/pleasure	moderate: 200–400 words per minute
for skimming	fast: 400–700 words per minute
for scanning	very fast: 700+ words per minute

Skimming is reading quickly to get a sense of the broad meaning of the article. We skim an article to see if the article is important to us. Naturally, comprehension can be low.

Scanning means you are looking for a specific piece of information without worrying about the broader meaning. You may be looking for a specific word or fact. Comprehension is also low.

Skimming and scanning work well when you know what you are looking for. You should not skim or scan a text if you need to comprehend and remember the material fully.

In small teams, search through the readings in this book to find answers to these trivia questions. The team that finds all the correct information first wins.

Team name: ....

Starting Time: .... Finishing Time: .... Elapsed Time (duration): ....

1. What was the first movie release to use Sensurround?
....

2. What is the pitch of a typical female voice? ....

3. What device or instrument features a bridge and a saddle?
....

4. What event does the National Sleep Foundation promote each year?
....

5. Did the Nasdaq stock exchange exceed 5,000 on March 10, 2000?
....

6. Which one of these is not a type of tulip—Semper Augustus, Charles II, Admiral Van Eyck, or Admiral Liefken? ....

7. What did the crowd think the ox weighed? ....

8. Without "googling" his name, identify the school that Larry Page attended.
....

You probably found much of the information more quickly than you thought you would. What tricks did you use to hunt down the answers?

VOCABULARY ACTIVITIES

Noun	Verb	Adjective	Adverb/ Conjunction
achievement	achieve	achievable	....
duration	....	....	....
element the elements	....	elemental elementary	elementally
excess	exceed	excessive excess	exceedingly excessively in excess of
maintenance	maintain	maintained	....
welfare	....	....	....

A. Read these comments on animal extremes. Fill in the blanks with a target word from the chart above that completes the sentence in a grammatical and meaningful way. Be sure to use the correct form.

1. The pronghorn antelope can .... speeds of 30–45 miles per hour over long distances.

2. The normal swimming speed of emperor penguins is 4–6 miles per hour, but they can .... speeds of more than 11 miles per hour in short bursts.

3. Emperor penguins can endure the extreme cold of Antarctica, where temperatures can reach -60°C (-76°F) for long ....

4. By huddling together, emperor penguins can survive the Antarctic winter's .... harsh conditions.

5. The bar-headed goose can reach heights in .... of 29,000 feet as it migrates over the Himalayas to its nesting ground in Tibet.

6. Racing homer pigeons are taken to a distant location and released to race home. They .... an average speed of about 30 miles per hour.

7. The National Wildlife Federation is concerned about the .... of animals.

8. The arctic hare has several adaptations that help it battle ....

B. Circle the alternative that best captures the meaning of the underlined target word in each sentence.

1. During the debate, the biologist <u>maintained</u> that humans are the best runners in hot weather.

   a. held his opinion   **b.** supported his opinion

2. The museum's collections are poorly <u>maintained</u>.

   a. cared for   **b.** argued for

3. The students found the demonstration <u>exceedingly</u> helpful.

   a. very   **b.** too

4. Some students complained that the amount of lab work was <u>excessive</u> and not very useful.

   a. fast-moving   **b.** unnecessarily great

5. The otter's thick, dense fur helps it endure the <u>elements</u>.

   a. weather   **b.** chemicals

6. To survive in cold weather, take these <u>elementary</u> precautions.

   a. basic   **b.** essential

7. One <u>element</u> of the arctic wolf's success is its ability to consume huge amounts of meat.

   a. small amount   **b.** part

The word *element* has many meanings, most related to the idea of something basic or fundamental.

a. a basic part of sth*	a key / necessary / essential / crucial / important *element*
b. the "basics" of a subject	the *elements* of bookkeeping, physics, computers, etc.
c. a subgroup of people	a violent / radical / moderate / questionable *element*
d. a small amount	an *element* of truth / risk / surprise
e. the weather	exposed to / protected from / battle the *elements*
f. chemistry	a chemical *element*, such as gold, mercury, or oxygen
g. electronics	a device that gets hot

*Note: *sth* is a common dictionary abbreviation for *something*

C. Which meaning of the word *element* is expressed in each sentence? Match each sentence with a definition in the box above. Compare answers with a partner.

.... **1.** There is an element of risk in any investment.

.... **2.** The heating element in the oven was replaced.

.... **3.** A key element of survival is being able to escape from predators.

.... **4.** The course introduces students to the elements of wildlife management.

.... **5.** The more vocal element in the group shouted down the speaker.

.... **6.** A thick coat of fur is necessary to protect arctic animals from the elements.

.... **7.** The heaviest, naturally occurring, non-radioactive element is bismuth.

D. Use information from Reading 1 to answer these questions in your notebook. Use the word or expression in parentheses in your answer.

1. How deep can the emperor penguin dive? (*a depth exceeding*)

2. What speed can pronghorn antelope travel over long distances? (*maintain*)

3. How fast can a peregrine falcon fly? (*achieve*)

4. What special ability do wildebeests, terns, and salmon have? (*long durations*)

E. Read this trivia about other record-setting animals. Restate each sentence using the word or phrase in parentheses. Be prepared to read aloud or discuss your sentences in a small group.

1. Blue whales can weigh over 170 tons. (*in excess of*)

2. The sounds made by blue whales can reach beyond 150 decibels. (*exceed*)

3. To survive, a squirrel must remember where it has individually hidden thousands of nuts. (*welfare depends on*)

4. Dall's porpoise, the fastest sea mammal, can travel up to 56 miles per hour. (*achieve speeds*)

5. The marmot, a large rodent, can hibernate for up to nine months a year. (*durations*)

BEFORE YOU READ

Read these questions. Discuss your answers in a small group.

1. Is physical fitness important for success in the modern world?
2. In Reading 1 we learned about animals that can outdo humans in many athletic categories. In what general athletic category(ies) do you think humans would excel?

MORE WORDS YOU'LL NEED

biomechanics: the biological mechanisms that allow animals to move

center of gravity: the point in a body or mass where the weight is most concentrated

counterweight: a weight that helps balance an object that would be too heavy on one side

torso: the upper body except for the head and arms; also called the trunk

READ

This science magazine article discusses how humans run, and the advantage that this ability has given us.

Were Humans Born to Run?

Compared to cheetahs, whose bursts of speed reach 70 miles per hour, or migrating wildebeests that roam over 2,000 miles a year, we humans must seem lead-footed homebodies.
5 As big as we are, we cannot seem to catch a cat or dog or even a chicken unless we can corner it or trick it.

But has our natural envy of a few fleet-footed species or our clumsiness in catching nimble
10 escape artists caused us to underestimate ourselves? University of Utah biologist Dennis Bramble and Harvard University paleoanthropologist[1] Daniel Lieberman think so. In fact, they maintain that decades
15 of research indicates that humans are very good runners indeed—perhaps the best in the world— when the distance gets long and the weather gets hot.

Hot to Trot

20 To understand how they can make this claim, let's consider what humans can do. The very best long-distance runners can run five-minute miles for several hours. These efforts are amazing achievements, but even the casual
25 jogger can often keep up an 8–10 minute a mile pace for several miles. Only a few animals of similar weight—large dogs, hyenas, wolves, and wildebeests—are capable of maintaining such speeds and actually prefer to trot a bit slower.
30 Even a thousand-pound horse will not cover long distances any faster than a good recreational jogger.

And in hot weather, humans may hold a decided advantage. One of the most incredible
35 feats of human endurance is the annual Badwater-to-Mt. Whitney run. The race begins in Death Valley, California, at an elevation

---

[1] *paleoanthropologist*: one who studies the biological history of human beings

285 feet below sea level, in July, the hottest month of the summer. The runners run 135
40 miles, crossing several mountain ranges with a cumulative elevation gain of 13,000 feet, and finish at an elevation of 8,360 feet at the Whitney Portal trailhead, about halfway up the 14,440-foot mountain. Each year approximately
45 75 men and women enter the race with 60–80% finishing within 60 hours and with the winning time usually well under 30 hours. Despite temperatures reaching 130°F,[2] there have been no fatalities so far. These men and women can
50 probably outrun any animal on the planet.

What makes it possible for these people to **undergo** such an ordeal? It turns out that humans are beautifully designed to run long distances in hot weather. Long-distance running
55 requires the ability to keep from overheating, and we humans have several advantages in this regard. First, we **release** heat by sweating through millions of sweat glands[3] rather than through panting. And because we have no
60 fur, our sweat evaporates quickly. Our upright posture also helps immensely by exposing less **area** to direct sunlight and more surface area to the cooling effect of the wind we create as we run. We excel at keeping cool, while most other
65 animals simply cannot shed heat fast enough to run long distances.

Humans can keep cool as they run.

But cooling is not enough to explain our speed over long distances. A second advantage is our long stride. When Professor Bramble filmed his
70 student David Carrier running alongside a horse moving at an easy gallop, he noticed that Carrier took fewer strides than the horse, indicating that Carrier's strides covered more distance than the horse's. Bramble was surprised by this
75 and began considering what elements of human biomechanics make this possible. Working with Lieberman at Harvard, he realized that humans, like horses and rabbits, can run without their heads bobbing up and down due to a piece of
80 anatomy, the *nuchal ligament*, which links the head to the spine. This tendon-like[4] band is not involved in walking, suggesting that it is a special adaptation important for a species that at one time needed to run, not walk, to find its dinner.

85 **A Spring in Our Step**

In fact, walking, it turns out, is a distinctively different motion than running. When walking, the heel hits the ground first, the leg straightens, and the body lurches forward a bit. As the
90 weight **transfers** to the ball of the foot, the arch stiffens and then pushes the body forward, with the other foot moving forward to keep the stride going. With running, the legs become large springs. You land more heavily on the arch of
95 the foot and bend your knee, which causes the body's center of gravity to lower. The force from this hard landing is captured by the tendons of the foot and leg, particularly the calf[5] muscles, and you spring forward as the tendons recoil.
100 According to Bramble, these huge, springy tendons are not necessary for walking.

Huge, springy tendons explain where the energy comes from, but how do humans maintain their balance and keep from falling
105 over? All other two-legged animals that run fast, such as kangaroos and roadrunners, have large tails that serve as a counterweight to keep the

---

[2] *130°F*: 130 degrees Fahrenheit, equals 54 degrees Celsius (54°C)
[3] *gland*: cells in the body that produce a specific substance
[4] *tendon*: a tough fiber that connects muscle to bone and other muscles
[5] *calf*: the back of the lower leg

animal balanced. Humans are obviously tailless, so how do they do it? Motion studies of runners
110 on treadmills offer clues. It seems we have a rather substantial rear end due to a large muscle, the *gluteus maximus*, that connects our hips to our lower back. This muscle does not do much when we walk, but it works very hard when
115 we run. Its role, it seems, is to act like a brake on our torso to keep it from lurching too far forward when our foot hits the ground.

Other anatomical **features** that **facilitate** running are our long necks and our shoulders.
120 We are able to twist our shoulders without moving our head, allowing us to pump our arms as another steadying mechanism that helps counterbalance our head and keep it upright.

Eat on the Run

125 There is no doubt, then, that humans are able to run, but why? Today most people are sedentary and run **solely** for pleasure or sport. Could it be that in our prehistoric past long-distance running was necessary for survival?
130 Sprinting fast allows an animal to drag down prey or escape a predator, but why would an ability to sustain a long run through hot weather be necessary? To hunt perhaps? But didn't prehistoric humans hunt by sneaking up on
135 animals and spearing or clubbing them? That certainly seems more efficient than chasing an animal for miles until it drops from heat

exhaustion. Or is our ability to run a byproduct[6] of some other ability? It seems running muscles
140 also help us stand up quickly and climb things, and certainly our springiness helps us fight more effectively.

Any conclusions we draw at this point are **preliminary**. But knowing that we can run long
145 distances may point us in the right direction for further study. It gives us clues as to how prehistoric humans lived. Perhaps adult hunters needed to travel long distances to track a herd and return before dark. Humans do not see
150 well at night and by running could extend their hunting range without constantly breaking camp and uprooting a family or village. Perhaps they did not hunt at all but needed to move quickly in order to reach prey killed by other animals
155 and join in on the feast. Could scavenging, as unsavory as it seems, be the sole reason for our running ability?

The debate undoubtedly will continue, with those who dislike sweaty activity naturally
160 skeptical of any prehistory that forced us to move out of the shade. But those eighty or so people who attempt the Badwater-to-Whitney run each year and the hundreds of thousands of people who enter the many 26.2-mile marathons
165 held in cities throughout the world make it difficult to deny the obvious—some humans, if not all, are definitely born to run.

---

[6] *byproduct*: something that happens as a result of something else

READING COMPREHENSION

Mark each sentence as *T* (true) or *F* (false) according to the information in Reading 2. Use the dictionary to help you understand new words.

......T...... 1. Humans have a unique way of running not found in other species.

.........F.. 2. The reading encourages the reader to get more exercise.

.........F.. 3. The reading sees running as a byproduct of walking.

.........F.. 4. The experts agree on the reasons prehistoric humans were such good distance runners.

.........T.. 5. The reading implies that most animals have trouble seeing clearly while they run.

READING STRATEGY: Outlining as You Read

> A good way to make sure you catch and understand the main points of a text is to *outline* it as you read. An outline is a diagram of the structure of the reading.

A. A simple outline shows the basic structure of the text. Complete this simple outline of Reading 1 on pages 3–4.

Introduction (Main idea: Some animals are capable of outstanding athletic performances.)

I. *Sprinting*

II. _____

III. *Diving*

IV. _____

V. _____

Closing Remarks

B. An outline can also have subheadings. Complete this more detailed outline of Reading 1 on pages 3–4. Be careful: the method of categorizing animals and animal achievements changes throughout the article.

I. Sprinting

   A. *Mammals*

   B. _____

II. Marathon

   A. _____

   B. _____

   C. _____

III. Diving

   A. _____

   B. _____

IV. Jumping

   A. _____

   B. _____

V. Weightlifting

   A. _____

   B. _____

C. When a formal outline is unnecessary or too difficult, you can take quick notes using bullet points and indentation. Look at how one student took notes for a short section of Reading 2 on pages 9–11. Then, in your notebook, make a quick outline of the key points of the whole text.

— *ways humans lose heat*
  — *millions of sweat glands release heat*
  — *Ho tur. Sweat evaporates quickly.*
  — *upright posture*
    — *less area exposed to the sun*
    — *more area exposed to cooling wind*

VOCABULARY ACTIVITIES

Noun	Verb	Adjective	Adverb
area	....	....	....
facilitation facilitator facility	facilitate	facilitating	....
feature	feature	featured featureless	....
preliminaries	....	preliminary	....
release	release	released	....
....	....	sole	solely
transfer	transfer	transferable	....
....	undergo	....	....

A. Read this information on other human abilities. Fill in the blanks with a target word from this unit (in the chart above or the chart on page 6) that completes the sentence in a grammatical and meaningful way. Words may be used more than once. Be sure to use the correct form.

Humans are impressive distance haulers, but to carry a load uphill successfully, your stride must (1) .... some changes. On flat surfaces, your calf muscles greatly (2) .... fast walking, providing forward push. You (3) .... momentum from one stride to the next by rocking forward as your back foot (4) .... from the ground. On a steep hill, this method quickly tires you out. To (5) .... a steady pace, lift one leg and plant it a short distance uphill. Straighten it while leaning slightly forward. Raise your back leg, but don't swing it forward until your front leg is straight. This method may sound slow, but your uphill speed and endurance will improve noticeably.

continued

One (6) .... where humans excel is throwing. In the
(7) .... stage of a throw, the arm moves up and back to capture
energy in the muscles of the shoulder, back, and legs. The torso moves slightly ahead
to build more energy. The arm then springs forward and (8) ....
energy to the object. Just before the (9) .... , the wrist and fingers
snap forward to add velocity. The best athletes can throw objects at speeds
(10) .... 100 mph.

**B. Which meaning of the word *feature* is expressed in each sentence? Match each sentence on
the left with a definition on the right. Compare answers with a partner.**

.... 1. The feature lasted nearly three hours.	**a.** an important part
.... 2. Her research featured strongly in the report.	**b.** parts of a face (usually plural)
.... 3. The car features a GPS navigation system.	**c.** a movie
.... 4. His rugged features helped him land many parts.	**d.** a special program or article
.... 5. The wandering albatross's most obvious feature is a wingspan of about 3.5 meters.	**e.** to include sth special
.... 6. They will run several features on endangered animals next week.	**f.** to play an important part

**C. The word *facilitate* means to make something easier to do. What tools or practices facilitate
these things?**

1. trade between countries

   A knowledge of local business practices can facilitate trade between countries.

2. learning a language

   ....

3. childhood development

   ....

4. keeping in contact with friends

   ....

5. the healing of a muscle injury

   ....

Collocations Chart

Verb	Adjective	Noun	Noun Compound
....	*elementary*	school, knowledge, laws, approach, mistakes, stage	....
....	*elemental*	truth, changes, force, aspect, characteristics, part, meaning	....
exceed	....	expectations, authority, limits	....
....	*excessive*	force, amount, noise, use, drinking, demands	....
....	*sole*	survivor, purpose, heir, authority, objective	....
....	*preliminary*	report, findings, remarks, research, results, inquiry, approval	....
promote, improve	social, personal, child	(the) *welfare* (of sth)	state, benefits, services, agency
undergo	....	change, operation, test, ordeal, transformation, examination, review, evaluation	....

D. The chart above shows some of the more predictable collocations, or word partners, for selected target vocabulary. Using the chart, complete these sentences with a likely word. Be sure to use the correct form.

1. The actress is devoted to promoting the .... of animals.

2. Last year, the company's policies .... an intensive review.

3. The .... purpose of the review was to find ways to cut costs.

4. The manager .... his authority when he fired the worker.

5. .... findings show the cause of the accident was human error.

6. The bridge collapsed under the pressure of .... weight.

7. He wanted to play basketball, but he had to face an .... truth: he would never be tall enough to play professionally.

8. Her love of animals began in .... school, when her class visited the zoo.

E. Build sentences using a random generator: Your teacher or partner calls out a random two-digit number to identify two words from the lists below. You then use those words to write a grammatical and meaningful sentence.

Teacher: "2-1." [The two words are "area" (2) and "exceed" (1).]

Possible sentence: "The area of the room exceeds 400 square feet."

0. achieve	0. preliminary
1. achievement	1. exceed
2. area	2. excessive
3. endure	3. exceedingly
4. endurance	4. maintain
5. element	5. release
6. elementary	6. welfare
7. facilitate	7. duration
8. sole	8. transfer
9. solely	9. undergo

WRITING AND DISCUSSION TOPICS

1. Many animals have amazing abilities that would make unlikely Olympic events. Do some research on one of these animals and write a paragraph describing what special skill or ability the animal has.

Archer fish (spitting)	elephants (hearing)
blue whale (largest appetite)	squirrels (memory)
eagle (eyesight)	tiger moths (navigating)

2. Exercise has its supporters and detractors. Two famous writers have very different attitudes toward exercise. Read the two quotes then explain which author's attitude is closer to your own.

   "It is exercise alone that supports the spirits and keeps the mind in vigor."

   — *Marcus Tullius Cicero, Roman statesman and philosopher (106–43 B.C.E.)*

   "I have never taken any exercise, except for sleeping and resting, and I never intend to take any. Exercise is loathsome."

   — *Mark Twain, American writer and humorist (1835–1911)*

3. Read this quote. Do you agree with the long-lived Santayana? Why or why not?

   "Exercise is a modern superstition invented by people who ate too much and had nothing to think about. Athletics don't make anybody either long-lived or useful."

   — *George Santayana, Spanish-American philosopher and novelist (1863–1952)*

4. Performing-enhancing drugs, some quite dangerous, are now a part of modern sports, and many sports heroes have been accused of using these substances. What should happen to an athlete caught using these substances?

YOUR ATTENTION, PLEASE

In this unit, you will

- ➲ read about research on two activities that affect human performance.
- ➲ learn to watch for "pivot" words to help find the main idea.
- ➲ learn to differentiate between cause and effect.
- ➲ increase your understanding of the target academic words for this unit:

benefit	evident	issue	negate	require
complex	identify	lecture	normal	research
consistent	instruct	mediate	psychology	whereas

SELF-ASSESSMENT OF TARGET WORDS

Think carefully about how well you know each target word in this unit. Then, write it in the appropriate column in the chart. When you've finished this unit, come back and reassess your knowledge of the target words.

I have never seen the word before.	I have seen the word but am not sure what it means.	I understand the word when I see or hear it in a sentence.	I have tried to use the word, but I am not sure I am using it correctly.	I use the word with confidence in either speaking or writing.	I use the word with confidence, both in speaking and writing.

BEFORE YOU READ

Read these questions. Discuss your answers in a small group.

1. Can you concentrate on two things at the exact same time? Try this: Think about the taste of ice cream while you add the numbers 71 and 56.

2. Picture in your mind the faces of two people you know. Can you see them at the same time, or do you switch back and forth?

3. Are you more productive when you work on a single project or when you work on several projects at the same time?

MORE WORDS YOU'LL NEED

motor skill: a physical skill that requires the use of muscles and bones

stimulus/stimuli (pl.): something that causes activity, development, or interest

READ

This article is about a behavior that seems to be increasing in our digital world.

"May I Have 30% of Your Attention, Please?"

Today it is possible to be productive, keep in constant contact with associates, and have fun at the same time. At least that is what ads for the latest digital gizmos[1] claim. While writing an
5 email to your boss or finishing a paper for your economics class, you can check for live updates on a tennis match halfway around the world or load songs into your portable media device. The boss expects you to prepare a sales report for
10 tomorrow's meeting. No problem. You can do it and read a movie review at the same time. Or can you?

Multitasking, the popular term for this behavior, originally referred to the process by
15 which computers appear to accomplish two or more tasks simultaneously. If computers can multitask with a single microprocessor, then certainly the much bigger human brain can train itself to do the same and enjoy the
20 **benefits** of increased productivity. We humans are quite adept at letting our minds wander while performing a routine motor skill. We can do the dinner dishes while thinking about our next vacation or chew gum while reading
25 a newspaper. But **psychologists** ask this question: Do multitasking humans operate effectively and efficiently when they really need to concentrate?

The **evidence** suggests that the answer
30 is no. One problem is interference, or what psychologists call the "Stroop effect." Back in the 1930s, the psychologist John Ridley Stroop showed there is a danger of error when the brain receives unexpected information while
35 carrying out a routine task. To see what he found, try this experiment on yourself:

As quickly as possible, say the name of each shape in Column 1 out loud. Then, do the same for Column 2. Then, do the same for Column 3.
40 If you are a good reader, most likely you completed the first column effortlessly, went a bit slower in the second column, and hesitated some, or even made an error, in the

---

[1] *gizmo*: gadget or small device

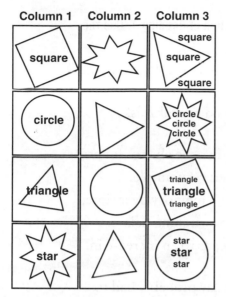

Column 1	Column 2	Column 3
square	(star shape)	square / square / square
circle	(triangle)	circle circle circle
triangle	(circle)	triangle **triangle** triangle
star	(triangle)	star **star** star

third column. Because you are much quicker at
45 reading words out loud than naming shapes, you
had difficulty ignoring the incorrect information
that you read. Of course, this drill is a bit
unnatural and designed to be confusing, but it
shows that multitaskers are vulnerable to error
50 and hesitation if they get interference from the
wrong set of stimuli while switching between
tasks. Imagine the damage a multitasking driver
or air traffic controller could do if incorrect
information intruded at the wrong time.

55　**Research** also suggests that switching between
tasks significantly delays completion. If the two
tasks are very routine and not too much alike—
say, humming along to a new tune while diapering
a squirming baby—the brain does not need to
60 switch between the tasks because the two require
different input channels. The humming requires
listening and singing, **whereas** the diapering
requires sight and the use of arm and hand
muscles. But when a similar kind of attention is
65 needed, the pace slows as the brain must switch
back and forth between the two tasks.

　In a study reported in the *Journal of
Experimental Psychology*, Rubenstein, Meyer
and Evans measured the amount of time lost
70 when people switch between tasks such as
solving math problems and **identifying** shapes.

They discovered that as the tasks become less
familiar, the area of the brain that **mediates**
task switching and assigns mental resources
75 takes longer to operate. Because each task
requires a different set of rules, it seems the
brain needs time to activate the appropriate
set. With **complex** tasks, the switching delays
add up, making multitasking less efficient than
80 concentrating on one task at a time. Other
researchers report that the brain shows less,
not more, neural activity when simultaneously
attempting two complex tasks even when a
different area of the brain is used for each task.
85 And less brain activity comes at a price. In one
study, subjects were **instructed** to write a report
and check their email. The multitaskers took
one and a half times longer than those who
completed one task before starting another.

90　This more leisurely work pace will no
doubt appeal to many. But the problems with
multitasking go beyond the **issue** of time
management. If switching takes time—perhaps
a half-second or more—that could be long
95 enough to distract a driver who is fiddling with[2]
a cell phone or scrolling through a complicated
digital display on a car dashboard. Constant
switching is also mentally stressful and may lead
to a diminished capacity to remember facts and
100 learn new skills. The brain simply may not get
the time it needs to build and maintain neural
connections and access memory.

　All these **negatives** do not mean that you
should never "whistle while you work" or sneak
105 a peak at a ballgame while studying chemistry.
But what about the boss who says "I need
that website up by Friday and can you take
my calls while I'm out" or the digital showoff
who sits through a university **lecture** while
110 text-messaging on a tiny cell phone screen and
nodding to the beat of music piped into barely
visible earphones? Remind them of this: The
multitasking machinery of our digital world was
most likely developed by very single-minded
115 people focused intently on a single task.

---

[2] *fiddle with*: make small adjustments to something restlessly or nervously

READING COMPREHENSION

Mark each sentence as *T* (true) or *F* (false) according to the information in Reading 1. Use the dictionary to help you understand new words.

.... 1. Some of the research on which this article was based predates the age of digital technology.

.... 2. The writer believes that the human brain can be trained to multitask effectively like a computer.

.... 3. Processing two sets of stimuli simultaneously diminishes the chance for error.

.... 4. Multitasking is possible when the tasks are routine and very simple.

.... 5. Multitasking can have detrimental effects on a person's memory over time.

.... 6. When multitaskers perform poorly, it is purely due to switching delays.

.... 7. Trying to do two complicated jobs at the same time leads to an increase in brain activity.

.... 8. The people who developed the digital tools we use today probably had to multitask in order to do so.

READING STRATEGY: Finding the Main Idea—Reading Past the "Pivot"

Writers can begin an article using several strategies. A news story might state the point of an article early, as in this example:

> A study reported in the *Journal of Experimental Psychology* reveals that <u>multitasking can actually waste time, especially when one of the tasks is complicated</u>. These findings are particularly relevant in an age when switching between tasks is greatly facilitated by digital technology.

Other articles might begin by providing background and context before getting to the main point or the real news featured in the article. They might even first present an idea that is counter to the true main point of the article. The transition or shift to the main idea is often indicated by a pivot word like, *but*, *yet*, *however*, or *nevertheless*, as in this paragraph:

> "Let's talk about this while we do the dishes." In the idiom of the digital world, we might call this an invitation to "multitask." The shared assumption? Dishwashing is so routine that even a serious discussion is possible while we finish the chore. **However**, <u>what happens when we try to do two tasks that require more intense concentration? Do we save time? Psychologists are beginning to have doubts.</u>

When looking for the main point of an essay, keep an eye out for these pivot words. Don't assume that the main idea of the article will always be stated in the first lines or even the first paragraph of the article.

A. Circle the pivot word in this paragraph. Underline the main idea.

Experimental psychology has a large body of work exploring how humans perform on repetitive or individual tasks requiring both cognitive and motor skills. Yet humans in daily life are often required to manage two or more tasks simultaneously. Our interest concerns how the human brain manages multiple tasks simultaneously and factors that inhibit the successful completion of these tasks.

B. Look again at Reading 1 and find a pivot. What information comes before the pivot? What information comes after the pivot? What point is the author making? Compare answers with a partner.

Pivot word: ....

Before pivot: ....

After pivot: ....

The author's point: ....

....

VOCABULARY ACTIVITIES

Noun	Verb	Adjective	Adverb/Conjunction
benefit beneficiary	benefit	beneficial	beneficially
complexity complex	....	complex	....
evidence	....	evident	evidently
identity identification	identify	identified identifiable	identifiably
instruction instructor	instruct	instructive instructional	instructionally
issue	issue	....	....
lecture	lecture	....	....
mediation	mediate	....	....
negative negativity	negate	negative	negatively
psychology psychologist	....	psychological	psychologically
requirement	require	required	....
research researcher	research	....	....
....	....	....	whereas

A. Read these comments on multitasking. Fill in the blank with a target word from the chart on page 21 that completes the sentence in a grammatical and meaningful way. Be sure to use the correct form.

1. Many in the working world today complain that multitasking is a

   .... for anyone who wants to get ahead.

2. Despite .... that multitasking wastes time, a great number of

   workers say they are expected to work on many tasks at once.

3. .... suggests that the human brain cannot match a computer's

   ability to switch back and forth between tasks.

4. An outside party was brought in to .... the dispute.

5. .... are interested in studying what the human brain is doing

   while multitasking.

6. Multitasking can be .... when tasks are routine and relaxing.

7. One .... effect of multitasking is a diminished ability to perform

   each task.

8. Researchers have found that learning new things has ....

   benefits for older people, improving their brain function and their outlook on

   life.

The noun *issue* refers to an important topic or problem for discussion. Academic
writing often involves the discussion of an *issue*.

The noun *issue* is often used with these verbs: *address, avoid, discuss, explore, raise.*

   To <u>explore</u> this **issue**, researchers conducted several experiments.

   There are several important **issues** that we must <u>address</u>.

   We wanted to <u>raise</u> the **issue**, but the writer is <u>avoiding</u> it.

B. Read the statements and identify an issue that each one might be addressing. Write a direct question that you could use to begin a discussion of the issue.

1. College tuition has been rising steadily.

   Issue: how people afford college ....

   What should we do about rising college tuition? or Why is college tuition rising? ....

2. Several factors have contributed to a decline in violent crime.

....

....

3. Raising the driving age to 17 will have several noticeable effects.

....

....

4. Students should be careful when posting personal information on social websites.

....

....

5. Parents need to monitor the violent content of video games more closely.

....

....

6. Disputes between workers and managers can damage businesses.

....

....

The conjunction *whereas* signals a contrast but it lacks the strong pivot feel of *but*, *yet*, *however*, and *nevertheless*, especially when it occurs in the middle of the sentence.

> *Humming requires listening and singing,* **whereas** *diapering requires sight and the use of arm and hand muscles.*

At the beginning of a sentence, *whereas* is more likely to signal a change in direction, or pivot point, in the main clause that follows. The word *while* behaves similarly.

> **Whereas** *humming requires listening and singing, diapering requires sight and the use of arm and hand muscles. It involves both the motor and visual regions of the brain...*

C. Here is an excerpt from Reading 2. Fill in the blanks with *whereas*, *but*, or nothing (*0*). Experiment with different possibilities. When you finish, compare sentences with a partner. How does the use of *whereas* or *but* affect the meaning?

Consistently failing to get enough sleep is the biological equivalent of consistently spending more money than you make. Napping can help reduce a sleep debt, (1) .... there are also long-term benefits to maintaining consistent, predictable sleep patterns. (2) .... naps do improve cognitive functioning after periods of sleep deprivation, (3) .... they do little to repair the negative mood that results from sleep loss.

Find the excerpt in paragraph 4 of Reading 2. How does it compare with your answers?

BEFORE YOU READ

Read these questions. Discuss your answers in a small group.

1. What is your typical sleeping schedule? Do you regularly take naps?
2. How much sleep do you need? Would you be more effective if you got more sleep?
3. The reading uses the term "sleep debt." What do you think it might mean?

MORE WORDS YOU'LL NEED

hormones: chemicals that are produced in the body and travel through the blood to send messages to different parts of the body

metabolism: the process by which living things change food into energy and materials for growth

READ

This article from the website of the American Psychological Association explains how more sleep would make most people happier, healthier, and safer.

You're Getting Very Sleepy

Findings

Many people are surprised to learn that researchers have discovered a single treatment that has many benefits. It improves memory,
5 increases concentration, strengthens the immune system, and decreases accidents. Sound too good to be true? It gets even better. The treatment is completely free, even for people with no health insurance. It also has no side effects. Finally, most
10 people consider the treatment highly enjoyable. Would you try it?

You probably should. For most people, this treatment **consists** of getting an extra 60–90 minutes of sleep each night. Both psychologists
15 and psychiatrists have maintained for years that Americans have overlooked one of the most significant public health problems—chronic[1] sleep deprivation. That is, few Americans regularly obtain the 8 or more hours of sleep
20 they require each night. The consequences of

chronic sleep deprivation can be truly disastrous. Laboratory experiments provide evidence that failing to get enough sleep dramatically impairs memory and concentration. It increases levels of
25 stress hormones and disrupts the body's **normal** metabolism. Research outside the laboratory further suggests that long-term sleep deprivation leads to greater susceptibility to motor vehicle accidents.

---

[1] *chronic:* constant

30 Research shows that many people are carrying a heavy "sleep debt" built up from weeks, months, or even years of inadequate sleep. In experiments on sleep debt, researchers pay healthy volunteers to stay in bed for at least 14 hours a day for a week
35 or more. Most people given this opportunity sleep about 12 hours a day for several days, sometimes longer. Then they settle into sleeping 7–9 hours per night. As William Dement put it, "this means … that millions of us are living a less
40 than optimal life and performing at a less than optimal level, impaired by an amount of sleep debt that we're not even aware we carry."

But is carrying a sleep debt really so harmful? Careful experiments by psychologist David
45 Dinges and others show that the answer is yes. Dinges and colleagues recruit healthy young volunteers who live continuously in Dinges's sleep laboratory for 10–20 days. Dinges randomly assigns them to receive different amounts and
50 patterns of sleep over time. He controls access to stimulants, such as caffeine, and constantly monitors the amount of sleep they get. Dinges has learned that people with fewer than 8 hours' sleep per night show pronounced cognitive and
55 physiological deficits. These deficits include memory impairments, a diminished ability to make decisions, and dramatic lapses in attention. As sleep deprivation continues, these deficits grow worse. Consistently failing to get enough
60 sleep is the biological equivalent of consistently spending more money than you make. Napping can help reduce a sleep debt, but there are also long-term benefits to maintaining consistent, predictable sleep patterns. Whereas naps do
65 improve cognitive functioning after periods of sleep deprivation, they do little to repair the negative mood that results from sleep loss.

Many people argue that they get by just fine on very little sleep. However, research shows that
70 few people can truly function well on less than 8

hours' sleep per night. Dinges estimates that, over the long haul, perhaps one person in a thousand can function effectively on 6 or fewer hours of sleep per night. Many people with chronic sleep
75 debts end up napping during the day or fighting off sleepiness in the afternoon. Moreover, people who chronically fail to get enough sleep may be cutting their lives short. A lack of sleep taxes the immune system and may even lead to disease
80 and premature aging. To make this worse, most people who are sleep deprived do not even realize it. If you get sleepy during long meetings or long drives, chances are you are chronically sleep deprived.

85 **Significance**

The National Highway Traffic Safety Administration estimates that drowsy or fatigued driving leads to more than 100,000 motor vehicle crashes per year. Even small disruptions in sleep
90 can wreak havoc on[2] safety and performance. In a nationwide study between 1986 and 1995, psychologist Stanley Coren studied the effects of the single hour of lost sleep that many Americans experience when they start daylight saving time[3].
95 The result? A 17% increase in traffic deaths on Mondays following the time change (compared with the Mondays before). Psychologists such as Gregory Hicks have observed similar findings. They focused specifically on alcohol-related
100 traffic related fatalities and observed increases in the week following the change to daylight saving time. It is harder to estimate the toll sleep deprivation takes on people's health, happiness, and productivity. But according to the National
105 Sleep Foundation, the annual loss in worker productivity due to sleeplessness is about $18 billion.

Practical Application

In light of[4] the dramatic public health
110 consequences of sleep deprivation and unhealthy

---

[2] *wreak havoc on*: cause damage to
[3] *daylight saving time*: the period of the year when the clock is turned one hour ahead to allow an extra hour of daylight
[4] *in light of*: informed by, due to

sleep patterns, the National Sleep Foundation (NSF) established National Sleep Awareness Week. In cooperation with partner organizations, this event is promoted each year during the
115 week when people set their clocks forward for daylight saving time. In 2003, the NSF reported that about 600 sleep centers in North America sponsored instructional activities in local communities during National Sleep Awareness
120 Week. Many U.S. states now educate drivers not only about the dangers of driving while intoxicated but also about the dangers of "driving while drowsy."

READING COMPREHENSION

Mark each sentence as *T* (true) or *F* (false) according to the information in Reading 2. Use the dictionary to help you understand new words.

.... 1. In David Dinges's experiment, the subjects stayed in bed for more than 14 hours a day.

.... 2. Research suggests that most people need more than 7–9 hours of sleep.

.... 3. It is the rare individual who can function effectively on fewer than 6 hours of sleep per night.

.... 4. If we are seriously deprived of sleep, a nap may help us think more clearly.

.... 5. Sleep deprivation affects not only a person's cognitive ability but also their mood.

.... 6. An enhanced immune system is one benefit of sleep deprivation.

.... 7. Studies have shown that people drink more when they are sleep deprived.

.... 8. Sleep deprivation is having an effect on the U.S. economy.

READING STRATEGY: Isolating Causes and Effects

Reading 2 uses the nouns *benefits* and *consequences* to signal that the reading is looking at the positive and negative effects of sleeping habits.

> There are long-term **benefits** to maintaining consistent, predictable sleep patterns.

> The **consequences** of this chronic sleep deprivation can be truly disastrous.

Writers can also use verbs to discuss effects more directly and describe specific positive or negative effects. Study the verbs in activity A for examples.

A. Reading 2 discusses the effects of two conditions—getting adequate sleep and chronic sleep deprivation. Without referring to the reading, mark the phrases *AS* (effects of adequate sleep) or *CD* (effects of chronic deprivation). Then, review the reading to check your answers.

.... improves memory

.... increases concentration

.... strengthens the immune system

.... decreases accidents

.... impairs memory

.... disrupts the body's metabolism

.... improves cognitive functioning

.... cuts their lives short

.... taxes the immune system

.... wreaks havoc on human safety

The verb *lead to* links a cause to its later effects. The verb *show* also describes an effect. The subject of the sentence is the *victim* or *beneficiary* of the effect.

Cause		Effect
Long-term sleep deprivation	*leads to*	...greater susceptibility to accidents
		...premature aging
		...disease
		...more motor vehicle crashes
People who get fewer than eight hours of sleep per night (victim)	*show*	...pronounced cognitive and physiological deficits
		...a diminished ability to make decisions
		...dramatic lapses in attention

B. Fill in the blanks with *lead to* or *show*.

1. Chronic sleep deprivation can .... pronounced cognitive and physiological deficits.

2. People who get less than 8 hours of sleep per night .... a greater susceptibility to motor vehicle accidents.

3. People who get adequate sleep .... improved cognitive functioning.

4. Not getting enough sleep can .... dramatic lapses in attention.

5. Getting adequate sleep .... improved memory.

6. According to laboratory experiments, people who are sleep deprived .... increased levels of stress hormones.

C. Referring to the reading and the preceeding tables, write a brief paragraph that summarizes the dangers of sleep deprivation.

VOCABULARY ACTIVITIES

Noun	Verb	Adjective	Adverb/ Conjunction
consistency inconsistency	.............................*	consistent inconsistent	consistently inconsistently
normal normality abnormality	normalize	normal abnormal	normally abnormally

* The verb *consist of* is treated in Unit 9.

A learner's dictionary typically has some information not found in a regular dictionary. Look up the words *evidence*, *research*, and *study*, for example. Find the [U] and [C] marks in the definitions. These are dictionary code for **count** or **uncount** nouns.

Count nouns can be plural (can be counted). Uncount nouns cannot be plural (cannot be counted). The words *evidence* and *research* are uncount. They cannot be plural and cannot be counted.

> **Research** <u>shows</u> that many people are carrying a heavy "sleep debt."

The noun *study*, like many nouns, can be count in one sense and uncount in another.

> **Studies** <u>show</u> that many people are carrying a heavy "sleep debt."
> The effect of sleep deprivation on highway safety deserves more **study**.

A. Read this information on sleep deprivation. Circle *C* (count) or *U* (uncount) for each underlined noun.

The National Sleep Foundation provides <u>information</u> (C / U) on the health <u>consequences</u> (C / U) of sleep deprivation. It offers practical <u>suggestions</u> (C / U) on how to get more sleep and <u>advice</u> (C / U) on how to take advantage of the <u>benefits</u> (C / U) that sleep provides. The organization believes that greater <u>knowledge</u> (C / U) and <u>understanding</u> (C / U) of sleep and sleep disorders will increase public <u>health</u> (C / U) and <u>safety</u> (C / U). To this end, it promotes the <u>study</u> (C / U) of sleep and sleep disorders.

The word *normal*—meaning "typical, as expected, ordinary"—can be a noun or adjective.

Here are some useful phrases:

return to *normal*	*normal* behavior
back to *normal*	*normal* conditions
below/above *normal*	*normal* development

The adjective *consistent* means "without much variation" or "without contradiction."

*The athlete is a **consistent** player.* (The athlete is dependable and predictable.)

*The witness's answers were **inconsistent**.* (The witness's answers changed or were contradictory.)

*Our results are **consistent** with other studies.* (We had similar or identical results.)

Here are some useful phrases:

consistent answers	*consistent* quality
consistent findings	*consistent* results
consistent pattern	*consistent* rules

B. Read this description of a crime. Then, discuss the questions that follow in a small group.

The sole employee of a small dress shop claimed that an armed robber stole all the cash while the owner was out running an errand. A few minutes before the owner returned, a witness sitting at a nearby café noticed a young man in a blue jacket leave the store and walk calmly but quickly away. The witness said he behaved normally, and there was nothing remarkable about his appearance.

The police then questioned the employee and collected these statements:

- I was cleaning the mirrors near the dressing rooms when the robber grabbed me from behind.
- He had a knife. I wanted to scream, but he had his hand over my mouth the whole time.
- He told me to take the money from the cash register and hand it to him.
- I gave him the money. He put it in a plastic bag and stuffed it in his jacket.
- He pushed me down and ran out before I could get a good look at him.
- The suspect's face was never toward me. I think he was very tall.
- I could not tell what color jacket the suspect was wearing.
- I know it was not a blue jacket.
- I didn't call the police because I wanted to wait for the owner.

1. Do you find the employee's statements logically consistent with each other or are they inconsistent?
2. Is there anything unusual or abnormal in the employee's behavior?
3. Are the employee's statements consistent with what the witness said?
4. Do you think the man in the blue jacket committed the crime? Why or why not?

C. Fill in the blanks with a target vocabulary word from the box. Use the plural form where necessary.

advice	information	suggestion
consequence	instruction	understanding
evidence	research	
fact	study	

1. The .... suggest that multitasking is only successful under limited circumstances.

2. The pamphlet offers several .... for people who have difficulty sleeping.

3. In the experiment, the subjects were asked to follow .... that were designed to be confusing and hard to follow.

4. One good piece of .... is to avoid caffeine before bedtime.

5. Multitasking can lead to errors if an incorrect piece of .... intrudes at the wrong time.

6. .... show that multitasking can delay the completion of tasks requiring concentration.

7. There is little .... that multitasking leads to greater productivity unless the tasks are routine and use different input channels.

8. Recent .... has raised some doubts about the efficiency of multitasking.

9. Psychologists now have greater .... of how the brain handles task switching than they did 15 years ago.

10. In some fields, multitasking can definitely have negative ....

D. The verb *identify* means to name or recognize something. To *identify* with someone means that you understand their feelings, thoughts, or values. Moviemakers want their audience to identify with the characters on screen. Which of these characters do you think are easy for people to identify with? Put a check (✓) next to them.

.... 1. a rebellious farm boy, bored with helping his aunt and uncle, who wants to fly spacecraft

.... 2. a smuggler who works for whichever side in a war pays him well

.... 3. a single mother who has fallen behind in her bills

.... **4.** an awkward high-school kid who falls in love with a girl who won't talk to him

.... **5.** a taxi driver without much ambition who is taken hostage

.... **6.** a pair of charming men who sneak into wedding receptions to take advantage of women

.... **7.** a successful 32-year-old woman who wants a family but works too hard to have time to date.

.... **8.** career criminals who want to steal something priceless and very well-guarded

In a small group, discuss your choices. Why are these characters easy to identify with? Why are the others not? What would need to happen in the story to make the audience identify with them?

Sentence Pattern Chart		
Target word	Pattern	Sample sentence
consistent	to be consistent with sth	His research on sleep is *consistent* with other studies.
evident	to be evident that…	It is now *evident* that multitasking has its limits.
evidence	there is evidence that… the evidence shows that…	There is little *evidence* that multitasking is more efficient. The *evidence* shows that multitasking can be inefficient.
require	to require sth to be required to do sth to require sth to do sth	Most adults *require* eight or more hours of sleep. They are *required* to perform several tasks at once. The boss *requires* us to do several jobs simultaneously.
benefit	to benefit from sth	Most adults could *benefit* from some more sleep.
beneficial	to be beneficial to do sth	It is *beneficial* to sleep.

E. Working with a partner, use these words to make a single sentence. Refer to the chart above for sentence patterns.

  1. evident / constant / beneficial

   The study claims that constant exposure to TV violence is not beneficial to a child's development.

  2. benefit from / psychological

  3. consistent with / research

  4. required / maintain

  5. evidence / negatively

  6. evident / beneficial

Collocations Chart

Verb	Adjective	Noun	Verb
derive, gain, receive, obtain, provide, offer	short-term, long-term, substantial, real	*benefits*	....
provide, cite, gather, look for	strong, direct, indirect, convincing, compelling	*evidence* that... *evidence* for sth *evidence* against sth	....
....	....	*evidence* *research*	suggests, shows, reveals, confirms, demonstrates that....
carry out, conduct, do	in-depth, extensive, ground-breaking, basic, original, ongoing	*research* on/into sth	....
....	*negative*	effect, attitude, mood, response, comment, consequence	....
meet, satisfy, fulfill, comply with, impose, waive, relax	strict, demanding, mandatory, basic, minimum	*requirements* (for sth or in order to do sth)	....

F. The chart above shows some common collocations, or word partners, for selected target vocabulary. Refer to the chart as you write sentences that contain the given words and at least one collocation.

1. strong / suggest / negative

    There is strong evidence suggesting that sleep deprivation has many negative effects.

2. fulfill / strict / in order to qualify for

3. provide / long-term

4. gather / compelling / against the claim that multitasking

5. carry out / on the negative / of chronic sleep deprivation

WRITING AND DISCUSSION TOPICS

1. An enterprising, ambitious student has a plan. This student hopes to get through college more quickly by sleeping only 4 hours a night and listening to tapes of lectures while studying for other classes. What do you think of this plan?

2. In what situations is multitasking an effective strategy for you? When is it ineffective?

3. Are people today expected to carry on too many activities at once? Or is multitasking simply a fact of life that all people must deal with?

4. "Eat right, exercise, and get plenty of rest." This common sense plan for achieving health is difficult to argue with, but many people struggle to follow this advice. Why is this advice so hard to follow?

MOVIE MAGIC

In this unit, you will

- ➲ read about pioneering special effects, some successful and some not.
- ➲ learn about annotating and highlighting.
- ➲ learn about verb tenses in a narrative or history.
- ➲ increase your understanding of the target academic words for this unit:

adjust	eventual	highlight	scheme	thereby
bond	final	margin	seek	vehicle
component	forthcoming	retain	subordinate	vision

SELF-ASSESSMENT OF TARGET WORDS

Think carefully about how well you know each target word in this unit. Then, write it in the appropriate column in the chart. When you've finished this unit, come back and reassess your knowledge of the target words.

I have never seen the word before.	I have seen the word but am not sure what it means.	I understand the word when I see or hear it in a sentence.	I have tried to use the word, but I am not sure I am using it correctly.	I use the word with confidence in either speaking *or* writing.	I use the word with confidence, both in speaking *and* writing.

BEFORE YOU READ

Read these questions. Discuss your answers in small groups.

1. All of the top 20 most popular movies of all time featured the latest in special effects. Are special effects the most important component in attracting a big audience?

2. Do you usually go to the theater to watch movies or do you watch them at home on DVDs or TV? Why? If you know that movie has a lot of special effects, will you be more likely see it in a theater?

3. Movies, to attract customers, often use advertising and promotional gimmicks to increase interest in a movie. What are some gimmicks that have been used to promote films?

MORE WORDS YOU'LL NEED

box office: the place in a theater where the tickets are sold. The term is often associated with the amount of money a movie earns

flop: fail (*v*), something that fails completely (*n*)

novelty: new and different

READING STRATEGY: Annotating and Highlighting

In Unit 1, you practiced outlining as a way of making notes about reading material. Two quicker methods for making notes involve writing directly on the book page. (Of course, this is only possible if the book is your own. You should never do this with library books or other books that don't belong to you.)

Annotating

Annotation means making notes in the margins of a reading. These brief notes identify key points or call out material that you may wish to reference later.

Highlighting

Highlighting means using a colored marker to draw attention to specific words, facts, or points in a reading. There are two ways to highlight text.

Indexing: Highlight key words and phrases to help find points and details later. It aids skimming and scanning. This approach is demonstrated in the second paragraph of Reading 1.

Summarizing: Highlight longer phrases to create a summary of the material. This approach is demonstrated in the third paragraph of Reading 1.

As you read the first three paragraphs of Reading 1, notice the annotation and highlighting that have been done for you. Add more if you want. Then, finish reading the article and do your own annotation and highlighting, using both the indexing and summarizing approaches.

READ

This magazine article discusses some of the best and worst special effects in cinematic history.

From Gimmicks to FX

Feature-length movies are expensive to make and must compete with other forms of entertainment—television, video games, sporting events, concerts—to attract and **retain** the large audiences they need to turn a profit. For this reason, moviemakers
5 endlessly **seek** new ways to bring audiences into theaters. Movies added sound and color in the late 1920s, widescreen formats in the early 1950s, and more recently advanced computer-generated-imaging to dazzle[1] us with increasingly elaborate special effects. Many of these special effects (FX) started out as "gimmicks" but
10 proved to be genuine advances that are now essential **components** of most big-budget movies. Other gimmicks have found their appeal more short-lived.

Some movie gimmicks don't last

One of the oddest gimmicks was the effort to add odors to the movie-going experience. If sound and **visual** images are possible,
15 then why not smell? As silly as it sounds, there were several serious attempts to enhance films with distinct aromas. In 1959, a film called *Behind the Great Wall* sent 50 odors through the air-conditioning system of a theater. For the 1960 film Scent of a Mystery, producer Mike Todd, Jr. (1929–2002) introduced "Smell-O-
20 Vision," a process designed to release carefully timed scents, such as pipe smoke or food, to each seat. Rather than launch Smell-O-Vision as the next evolution in entertainment, the film flopped. Mr. Todd, Jr. lost all his investment, and after that both he and Smell-O-Vision were out of the movie business.

Gimmick: add odors

"Smell-O-Vision" —flopped

25 Another group of less expensive gimmicks came from a small-time movie producer and director who actually did make money. To attract audiences to his low-budget horror films, William Castle (1914–1977) tried various **schemes** to convince people that his movies were scary. For *Macabre* (1963), he offered free $1,000 life
30 insurance policies in case the viewer died of fright. For his film *The Tingler*, he equipped selected seats with the "Percepto," a device that gave an electronic jolt to patrons at crucial points in the film. This jolt would cause the patron to scream, **thereby** adding to the tension in the theater. Castle is perhaps best remembered for
35 "Illusion-O," a device he used in the movie *Thirteen Ghosts*. He supplied each customer with handheld "ghost glasses" that would

William Castle—less expensive gimmicks.

"Percepto"—shocks in seat

"Illusion-O"—ghost glasses

---

[1] *dazzle*: amaze

allow the user to see the ghosts and remove them if they became
"too frightening." Since everyone would most likely want to see the
40 ghosts, the device seems pointless. Why not just show the ghosts?
But the gimmick was intended to be fun and increase anticipation
that the ghosts were going to be a lot scarier than they actually
were. In practice, most of Castle's gimmicks were only **marginally**
successful and often got more giggles than screams—an inflatable[2]
45 skeleton floating above the audience during *House on Haunted Hill*
(1959) became a target for thrown candy boxes and soda cups—but
his movies were entertaining and made money. In fact, *Thirteen
Ghosts* received a big-budget remake in 2001. This time, though,
only the actors got to wear the ghost glasses.

50   Advertising for the 1975 movie *Earthquake* **highlighted**
Sensurround Sound, promising sound that was powerful enough
to "crack ribs." The effect of a low-pitched earthquake rumble was
achieved by placing up to ten large subwoofer[3] speakers around the
theater wired to a powerful amplifier. When cued by signals in the
55 film, the speakers emitted a powerful vibration that was felt more
than heard. Unlike Smell-O-Vision and Castle's inexpensive tricks,
the problem with Sensurround was that it was too successful. Since
more and more theaters were multiplexes[4], the vibrations bothered
patrons in adjacent theaters watching different films. Complaints
60 by patrons and reports of damage to theaters convinced most
theater owners that Sensurround was not worth the trouble.
Only three more films—*Midway* (1976), *Rollercoaster* (1977), and
Battlestar Galactica (1978) featured the effect.

    The most famous special effect, one that reappears frequently
65 and is still being improved on, is the movie in 3-D. Studios had
experimented with three-dimensional photography as far back
as 1922, but the first hit 3-D movie was *House of Wax* in 1953. This
visual effect is achieved by sending a slightly different image
to each eye. For this to occur, the moviegoer must wear special
70 glasses that eliminate the image that the other eye is seeing. This
technique was successful enough that from 1953 to 1955 studios
released dozens of 3-D movies. However, the process was not
immune from technical glitches (patrons complained of eyestrain)
and **eventually** the novelty wore off. From 1955 on, 3-D movies
75 became less common, with the technology mainly associated with
nonfiction IMAX[5] releases.

---

[2] *inflatable*: designed to be filled with air or gas before use
[3] *subwoofer*: a speaker that emits a very low-pitched sound
[4] *multiplex*: a movie complex that contains many individual theaters
[5] *IMAX*: a film format used for films shown on very large screens

Inflatable skeleton in theater

Movies made money

It is tempting to look at a box-office loser like Smell-O-Vision and mutter "What were they thinking?" But the other short-lived gimmicks were actually associated with box office successes. And today, 3-D technology is being revived and improved upon, with
80 many new releases **forthcoming**, particularly now that the large-screen IMAX theaters are moving into fiction films. And watch out. Be ready for a movie so terrifying that moviegoers are advised, "Check with your cardiologist before seeing this film."

READING COMPREHENSION

A. Mark each sentence as *T* (true) or *F* (false) according to the information in Reading 1. Use the dictionary to help you understand new words.

.... **1.** After the failure of Smell-O-Vision, Mike Todd, Jr. went on to make other movies.

.... **2.** William Castle is still making movies.

.... **3.** Castle's special effects gimmicks were not entirely successful.

.... **4.** One problem with Sensurround was that it caused injuries to movie goers.

.... **5.** The most promising of the FX discussed is 3-D movie technology.

.... **6.** Many viewers found that the glasses used for 3-D movies hurt their eyes.

.... **7.** The reading suggests that moviegoers today are too sophisticated to fall for FX and gimmicks.

.... **8.** The article suggests that most special effect gimmicks were complete failures.

.... **9.** Some movies are so scary that viewers need to check with their doctors before they go.

B. Scan the article for the answers to these questions. First think about the key word you will scan for. Use your annotation and highlighting to help you. Compare answers with a partner.

1. What was the name of the thing that enabled people to see ghosts in a movie?

    Key word: *ghost*

    Answer: *It was the Illusion-O.*

2. Is William Castle still alive?

3. What kinds of odors were used in the Smell-O-Vision movies?

4. What was the first hit 3-D movie?

5. Which four films featured Sensurround?

6. Which movie had a big-budget remake in 2001?

VOCABULARY ACTIVITIES

Noun	Verb	Adjective	Adverb/ Conjunction
component	....	component	....
eventuality	....	eventual	eventually
....	....	forthcoming	....
highlight	highlight	highlighted	....
margin	marginalize	marginal	marginally
retention	retain	retentive	....
scheme a schematic	scheme	scheming schematic	schematically
....	seek	sought-after	....
....	....	....	thereby
vision a visionary	envision	visual visionary	....

A. Read this article on recent developments in 3D technology. Fill in the blanks with a target word from the chart that completes the sentence in a grammatical and meaningful way. Be sure to use the correct form.

The original 3-D movie technology had several drawbacks. First, it required special glasses. Even with these, the image was often out of focus, causing eyestrain. Second, the effect would only work in the area directly ahead of the screen. However, the human field of (1) .... extends well beyond the (2) .... of the screen. Therefore, unless the viewer sat in the middle of the theater, the effect did not work well. (3) ...., the novelty lost its ability to (4) .... audience interest, and box office sales dropped.

With new technology developed by IMAX and other companies, successful 3-D movies are soon (5) .... The huge IMAX screens solve the field of vision problems. 3-D IMAX versions of animated films have already attracted customers, particularly a 3-D version of *The Polar Express* (2004). Along with the rapid development of HDTV technology and computer-generated imaging, high-tech firms are working on innovative (6) .... for achieving 3-D effects on a two-dimensional screen. One technique involves a screen with tiny angled ridges that send a different image to each eye. This development would eliminate the most annoying (7) .... of the 3-D viewer's experience, the glasses.

B. The words in bold can have different meanings. Find the phrases in Reading 1 and circle the meaning appropriate to this context.

1. ... **marginally** successful
   - **a.** along a side border
   - **b.** slightly

2. ... tried various **schemes**
   - **a.** tricky or secret plans
   - **b.** ways of arranging things

3. ... many new releases **forthcoming**
   - **a.** cooperative and informative
   - **b.** coming in the near future

4. ... attract and **retain** large audiences
   - **a.** keep, continue to have
   - **b.** hire for a fee

5. ... **highlighted** Sensurround Sound
   - **a.** emphasized
   - **b.** marked with a special color

The noun *vision* and its verb form *envision* relate to seeing, physically and mentally.	
eyesight	blurred / good / perfect / poor / unobstructed / 20–20 *vision*
a clear view of future possibility	a global / clear / common / personal *vision*
mental picture	a disturbing / bleak / prophetic / religious *vision*
a supernatural experience	a religious / ghostly / otherworldly / mystical *vision*
picture mentally	*envision* difficulties / a future / a plan / possibilities / problems

C. Which meaning is expressed in each sentence? Match the sentence on the left with the definition on the right. Compare answers with a partner.

.... **1.** She was praised for the clear vision she has for the company's future.

a. eyesight

.... **2.** He envisioned better times ahead.

b. a view of future possibility

.... **3.** Humans have poor color vision at night.

c. mental picture

.... **4.** She has a bleak vision of her future in the movie business.

d. a supernatural experience

.... **5.** A ghostly vision appeared before him.

e. picture mentally

BEFORE YOU READ

Read these questions. Discuss your answers in a small group.

1. Have you ever created a special effect of any kind? What was it? How did you create it?

2. What kind of personality, talent, and training would make someone good at creating movie special effects?

3. In 2004, *Lord of the Rings: Return of the King* earned the Academy Award for Best Picture. Until then, no movie featuring fantastic creatures or monsters had ever won this prestigious award. Are movies in the fantasy, science fiction, and horror categories underrated? Why do you think these movies rarely win the big awards?

MORE WORDS YOU'LL NEED

blockbuster: a hit movie, usually one with a big budget and an epic story

Oscar: the nickname of an award given by the Academy of Motion Picture Arts and Sciences, also called an Academy Award

READ

This article describes the work of Ray Harryhausen, special effects visionary. Annotate and highlight as you read.

A Big Gorilla Started It All

King Aeetes of ancient Greece is desperately seeking the Golden Fleece. Only Jason and his men stand in his way.[1] He reaches into a helmet and throws the Hydra's[2] teeth upon the ground.
5 Seven armed skeletons pop from the earth and march in unison toward three nervous warriors. "Kill them all," Aeetes cries. For nearly four minutes, a wild battle ensues among the ruins of a temple overlooking the sea, as three live actors
10 do close combat with the animated figures.

This famous action sequence from the movie *Jason and the Argonauts* (1963) is the work of special effects creator Ray Harryhausen, a legend and an inspiration to the technical
15 wizards who create the cinematic wonders we enjoy today. Those familiar with his work will

Live actors battle animated skeletons.

detect the influence of what he called "kinetic[3] sculptures" on later blockbuster films such as *Jurassic Park* and the *Lord of the Rings* trilogy.
20 Harryhausen achieved the skeleton illusion by using a technique called stop-motion

[1] In Greek mythology, Jason sets sail on his ship, the *Argo*, to find the golden fleece (wool) from a winged goat
[2] *Hydra*: (Greek mythology) a serpent-like beast with multiple heads
[3] *kinetic*: involving or resulting from motion

animation. Harryhausen equipped one-foot-tall model skeletons with joints that allowed the skeletons to move naturally. He photographed the skeletons in one pose. He then adjusted their bodies slightly and photographed them again. When this process was repeated many times and run as a movie, it created the illusion that objects were moving on their own. By coordinating the actions of the models with the actions of live actors, Harryhausen made us believe the miniature models were interacting with full-size human actors. It was a tedious process—the skeleton battle took 4½ months to film. But the characters were far more realistic and three-dimensional than cartoon characters and more physically expressive than puppets.

Born in Los Angeles, California, in 1920, Ray Harryhausen's **bond** with movie special effects formed at age thirteen when he saw the pioneering stop-motion work of Willis O'Brien in the film *King Kong* (1933). Even as an adolescent, Harryhausen could tell that the gigantic gorilla was not a man in an ape suit or a cartoon. He wondered how the filmmakers made the gorilla's movements seem so natural and its face so expressive.

Harryhausen began his long career of trying to achieve and surpass the effects made famous by *King Kong*. His first effort was a cave bear made out of his mother's fur coat and photographed with a borrowed camera. Despite difficulty controlling the camera, he succeeded in making the bear appear to move. Excited by the possibilities, he then sought training in all aspects of trick photography. He studied drawing, ceramics, and sculpture, each an important component in the success of his stop-motion work.

By 1940, Harryhausen was making films on his family's back porch and soon worked on animated shorts for Paramount Studios. In 1942, he was drafted into the Army Signal Corps where he worked on animated sequences for training films. After his discharge, Harryhausen made five stop-motion fairy tales called *Mother Goose Stories*. The artistic success of these animations led to his first big break when Willis O'Brien hired him to work on *Mighty Joe Young* (1949). The movie, an entertaining *King Kong* sequel of sorts, earned its producers a special effects Oscar.

In the 1950s, Harryhausen did impressive special effects work on low-budget, black-and-white science fiction monster films. In *The Beast from 20,000 Fathoms* (1953), sci-fi fans saw a giant, stop-motion dinosaur attack New York. In *It Came from Beneath the Sea* (1955), an octopus tears down San Francisco's Golden Gate Bridge. In *20 Million Miles to Earth* (1957), a monster from Venus grows huge and lays waste to Rome.

Over the next 24 years, Harryhausen turned from sci-fi to fantasy/adventure stories filmed in color. These ten films feature dozens of fascinating monsters, each a testament to Harryhausen's vision. In *The Seventh Voyage of Sinbad* (1958), live actors fight a giant two-headed bird, a 30-foot-tall Cyclops, and a living skeleton. In *Mysterious Island* (1961), castaways do battle with a gigantic crab and a huge bird. *Jason and the Argonauts* features a blind man fighting off two bird-like humans, a battle with a huge bronze man filled with thousands of gallons of fluid, and Jason's duel with a seven-headed hydra. And don't forget those relentless skeletons. Harryhausen's **final** feature film, *The Clash of the Titans* (1981), finds Perseus, the hero of Greek myth, fighting giant scorpions, outsmarting the deadly, snake-haired Medusa, and bringing down the colossus Kraken. Movie fans still marvel at the expressiveness and personality of these creatures.

Harryhausen was never nominated for a special effects Oscar. Some feel it was because he worked away from Hollywood on lower budget films, rarely using assistants. (Harryhausen retained close bonds with his family—his father made the ball and socket joints for his models and occasionally his mother made the fur coverings.) Others feel that until the success of George Lucas's *Star*

Wars (1977), Hollywood marginalized sci-fi movies, particularly those featuring monsters and strange creatures. In 1992, Hollywood
115 finally recognized this oversight[4] and honored Ray Harryhausen with a lifetime achievement Oscar. At the presentation ceremony, two-time Academy Award-winning actor Tom Hanks reportedly said to Harryhausen, "Lots of people
120 say *Citizen Kane* is the greatest film of all time.... No way, it's *Jason and the Argonauts*!"

Today, Harryhausen's stop-motion animation technique has been superseded by more sophisticated computer-generated imaging
125 and performance-capture animation[5]. People accustomed to seamless digital effects may find his work a little rough around the edges[6]. Nonetheless, many contemporary filmmakers are students of his work and cite it as their
130 inspiration. Peter Jackson, the director of the *Lord of the Rings* trilogy and *King Kong* (2005), is one prominent example. He credits much of his lifelong desire to make movies to a childhood fascination with Harryhausen's work. And most
135 of the stop-motion master's work, even his early experiments, is available on DVD today.

Movies are usually labeled as the work of the actors or director. Technicians most often play an unseen or **subordinate** role in the
140 moviegoer's mind. Ray Harryhausen defies that tradition. Although he never directed or acted in the 15 or so feature-length films he worked on, these films are now seen as **vehicles** for showcasing his talents. Known today as
145 "Ray Harryhausen films," each one is marked by the taste, imagination, and kinetic magic Harryhausen brought to his creations.

---

[4]*oversight*: mistake
[5]*performance-capture animation*: a technique that can digitally record a live actor's performance and use that data to animate another character
[6]*rough around the edges*: unpolished, unrefined

READING COMPREHENSION

A. Mark each sentence as *T* (true) or *F* (false) according to the information in Reading 2. Use the dictionary to help you understand new words.

.... 1. The movie about Jason was based on an ancient tale from Greek mythology.

.... 2. Ray Harryhausen was the first to have success using stop-motion animation.

.... 3. Ray Harryhausen tended to work alone on his stop-motion photography.

.... 4. Some feel that Hollywood didn't take sci-fi movies seriously in the years before *Star Wars*.

.... 5. Harryhausen had the support of his family in advancing his career in special effects.

.... 6. Stop-motion animation is not as smooth as computer-generated animation.

.... 7. Filmmakers today who specialize in special effects don't care about Harryhausen's work.

.... 8. Today it is difficult to find copies of Harryhausen's work.

B. Scan the reading for the answers to these questions. Use your annotation and highlighting to help you.

1. How does stop-motion animation work?
2. What has replaced stop-motion animation today?
3. What are three of the black-and-white films Harryhausen worked on?
4. What are three of the color films Harryhausen worked on in the late 1950s and early 1960s?
5. Who directed *Lord of the Rings*?
6. In which category did Harryhausen win an Oscar (Academy Award)?
7. About how many feature length films did Harryhausen work on in his career?
8. Who did the stop-motion animation in the 1933 film *King Kong*?

READING STRATEGY: Uses of the Present Tense

When describing actual historical events, writers typically use the past tense.

> Born in Los Angeles, California, in 1920, Ray Harryhausen's bond with movie special effects **formed** at age thirteen when he **saw** the pioneering stop-motion work of Willis O'Brien in the film King Kong (1933).

When summarizing or describing a story or setting, however, writers often use the present tense.

> King Aeetes of ancient Greece **is seeking** the Golden Fleece. Only Jason and his men **stand** in his way. He **reaches** into a helmet and **casts** the Hydra's teeth upon the ground.

When writers comment on or analyze a circumstance that still holds true, they can use the present tense. The present tense verb feature makes such a comment.

> Over the next 24 years, Harryhausen turned from sci-fi to fantasy/adventure stories filmed in color. These ten films **feature** dozens of fascinating monsters, each a testament to Harryhausen's vision.

Note: these are not strict rules and writers can use different verb tenses to create different effects. In the examples above, it would not have been wrong for the writer to use the past tense.

This paragraph describes software that can generate real-looking animated characters in movies. As you read, complete the sentences with either the past or the present tense. Compare work with a partner.

In *Jason and the Argonauts*, Ray Harryhausen (1. *use*) .... miniature models and stop-motion animation to create a realistic-looking battle where seven skeletons moved and reacted individually. But stop-motion animation (2. *have*) .... limits. The process is too slow to animate more than a few creatures at once.

Director Peter Jackson (3. *face*) .... this problem in the *Lord of the Rings* movies. The plot (4. *call*) .... for battles between thousands of fantasy characters. But no movie had ever succeeded in making that many animated characters look real. Jackson called on Stephen Regelous, an expert on visual effects and computer animation, to find a software solution. Regelous (5. *create*) .... a software application called Massive that can fill a scene with individual beings, or "agents." In stories animated with this software, these agents (6. *move and behave*) .... independently.

With this software, films can now add pre-built agents, such as people walking and talking on a city street. Artists also (7. *design*) .... their own creatures and individually (8. *animate*) .... them with Massive. Peter Jackson's *King Kong* (2005), for example, (9. *use*) .... Massive to fill Skull Island with animated insects, bats, and other creatures. For the New York scenes, Massive (10. *crowd*) .... the streets of Manhattan with moving cars, buses, and pedestrians.

Look again at the verbs you added in the passage. Write *H* next to those that describe a historical event. Write *C* next to those that comment on present circumstances.

VOCABULARY ACTIVITIES

Nouns	Verbs	Adjectives	Adverbs
adjustment	adjust	adjustable adjusted well-adjusted	....
bond bondage	bond	bonded	....
finality	finalize	final	finally
subordinate	subordinate	subordinate	....

A. These words can have different meanings depending on context. Scan Reading 2 to find which sense was intended and circle it here.

1. adjust

   a. raise or lower slightly   **b.** adapt, get used to   **c.** move sth slightly

2. subordinate

   a. secondary, less important   **b.** make less important   **c.** an assistant

3. final

   a. definitive   **b.** an examination   **c.** last in a series

4. vehicle

   a. means of transportation   **b.** instrument, tool, means

---

When a verb is followed by an object, it is called a *transitive verb*.

   *The glue can **bond** <u>metal</u> to wood.*

When a verb does not have an object, it is called an *intransitive verb*.

   *After moving here, she **adjusted** quickly to her new life.*

Most dictionaries will tell you whether a verb can be transitive, intransitive, or both. Depending on which dictionary you use, this can be indicated as follows:

Transitive	*v.t.*; *v.tr.*; *trans.*; [T]; [VN] (meaning <u>V</u>erb + <u>N</u>oun)
Intransitive	*v.i.*; *v. intrans.*; [I]; [V] (meaning no noun after verb)

B. You can learn a lot about a verb by studying how it is used in a sentence. Here are selections from the readings in units 1 and 2. Study the bold verbs and write *T* (transitive) or *Int* (intransitive) in the blank. For transitive verbs, underline the object. Compare work with a partner.

..*T*.. **1.** ...in order to eat, **seek** and catch <u>prey</u>, mate...

.... **2.** Why does it **run** so fast?

.... **3.** ...the cheetah can **outrun** its fleetest prey.

.... **4.** ... escape predators, and **endure** the elements

.... **5.** The pronghorn antelope has been **clocked** at close to 70 mph.

The word *bond* can be a noun or verb. It has many different meanings.

a strong connection, emotionally or physically	strong / common / close / emotional / parental *bond(s)* form / break / feel / forge / strengthen / destroy a *bond(s)*
a type of financial investment (usually plural)	savings / government / long-term / treasury *bonds* purchase / buy / sell / invest in / put money into / issue / redeem *bonds*
a joining of atoms into molecules/to form molecules	a chemical *bond* to chemically *bond*
a legal contract or promise	*A marriage is a legal bond.*
sth that restrains sb*	*The prisoner broke free from his bonds.*
to join firmly/to attach to	*This glue bonds well to most surfaces.*
to develop a strong trust in	*Ducklings will bond with the first animal they see.*

*Note: *sb* is a common dictionary abbreviation for *somebody*

C. Which meaning of the word *bond* is expressed in each sentence? Match the sentence on the left with the definition on the right. Compare answers with a partner.

.... 1. Despite different approaches, the software engineer and the graphic artist bonded immediately.

.... 2. Although born in Southern California, Harryhausen never developed a strong bond with Hollywood.

.... 3. Jack breaks free from his bonds and rejoins the crew of the *Black Pearl*.

.... 4. She put most of her wealth into stocks and bonds.

.... 5. He used a strong glue to bond the neck of the guitar to the body.

.... 6. Water is formed when specific amounts of hydrogen and oxygen bond.

.... 7. Paternity establishes a legal bond that protects the child.

a. a strong connection, emotionally or physically

b. a type of financial investment

c. the joining of atoms into molecules

d. a legal contract or promise

e. sth that restrains sb

f. to join firmly

g. to develop a strong trust in

Collocations Chart

Verb	Adjective	Noun
make, need	fine, minor, slight, small, major, significant	*adjustment*
....	strong, emotional, close, tight, common, special	*bond* (between / among...)
....	main, key, basic, major, central, core, vital, important, essential	*component*
....	*final*	report, decision, payment, analysis, outcome, approval, chapter, exam
....	*forthcoming*	appearance, book, election, talks, movie, events
retain	a copy, control, power, moisture, water, a title (sports), a job, the ability to do sth	....
devise, come up with, think up, carry out	grand, elaborate, brilliant, ingenious, ambitious, crazy	*scheme* (to do sth)
....	*subordinate*	role, position, rank, clause
have, develop, convey, impose	clear, grand, mental, flawed, shared, narrow	*vision* (of sth)

D. The chart above shows some common collocations, or word partners, for selected target vocabulary. Refer to the chart and complete these sentences. Compare work with a partner.

1. After the preview, they made some minor .... to the film's soundtrack.

2. In the interview, the director talked about the use of performance-capture technology in her .... movie.

3. He preferred to work alone, an arrangement that allowed him to .... complete artistic control.

4. Some critics complain that in current films, story and characterization play a .... role to special effects.

5. Innovative special effects were a vital .... of the film's success.

6. Observers could not agree on whether her plan showed a clear .... of the future or whether it was a crazy .... certain to fail.

7. The committee said that its decision was ....

8. A special .... developed among the people on the staff.

WRITING AND DISCUSSION TOPICS

A. Write a group story:

- Each student in a small group is assigned one set of words from the box. On a loose piece of paper, write the first line of a story featuring a word from your set of words.
- Pass your paper to the left and receive a paper from the right.
- Using another word from your set, continue the story you just received.

Continue this process until you have added to every story. Read the stories aloud.

1	2	3	4
achieve	element	release	transfer
welfare	duration	facilitate	preliminary
negate	require	complex	identify
instruct	mediate	psychology	whereas
vehicle	bond	final	retain
scheme	thereby	endurance	excessive
evidence	adjustment	margin	marginalize
5	6	7	8
undergo	exceed	maintain	sole
lecture	benefit	consistent	issue
adjust	eventual	research	evident
subordinate	vision	highlight	seek
achievement	sole	component	forthcoming
facility	endure	beneficial	complexity

Tip: You are writing a story, so put a character into the first sentence. That will help the next writer carry on the plot.

B. Discuss or write in response to these items.

1. Video games today make use of computer generated images and performance-capture animation to make the characters look real and move realistically in fascinating settings. Yet, some games, despite wonderful graphics, flop. What components contribute to the success of a video game?

2. Choose a recent blockbuster movie. Then search the movie's website, the bonus features on the DVD, or other sources to find information about the special effects employed. What technologies were used? Were any innovative techniques used?

3. "The best special effect is one the audience did not know was a special effect." What do you think this means? Do you agree or disagree with this statement?

4. Go online and do a search for "movie special effects." Find a technique that was **not** mentioned in this unit. Find out how it is done, how and where it is (or was) used, and interesting facts or stories about it. Present your research to the class.

THE POWER OF MUSIC

In this unit, you will

- ⇨ read about how the brain responds to music and how guitars are made.
- ⇨ learn about some features of technical description.
- ⇨ increase your understanding of the target academic words for this unit:

confer	fundamental	manipulate	project	theory
diminish	incorporate	physical	refine	transmit
foundation	intrinsic	prime	stress	

SELF-ASSESSMENT OF TARGET WORDS

Think carefully about how well you know each target word in this unit. Then, write it in the appropriate column in the chart. When you've finished this unit, come back and reassess your knowledge of the target words.

I have never seen the word before.	I have seen the word but am not sure what it means.	I understand the word when I see or hear it in a sentence.	I have tried to use the word, but I am not sure I am using it correctly.	I use the word with confidence in either speaking *or* writing.	I use the word with confidence, both in speaking *and* writing.

BEFORE YOU READ

Read these questions. Discuss your answers in small groups.

1. All cultures have music, but cultures and individuals disagree on what sounds good. Is there any kind of music that sounds good to most people?

2. What kind of music do you like most? What makes this music interesting to you?

3. Do you think there will someday be a pill that can make people more creative? Would you take it?

MORE WORDS YOU'LL NEED

auditory: related to hearing
circuitry: a system of electrical pathways (such as neural pathways in the brain)
pitch: the highness or lowness of a musical note
quasi-: prefix meaning "seemingly" or "partially" so

READ

This article reports some of the recent findings concerning the connection between emotional reactions to music and biology.

Why Does Music Move Us?

Science gets closer to the intersection of biology and creativity

Researchers are only now beginning to unlock the secrets of the brain. It seems like every month some new study or another comes along to explain why we get addicted to nicotine, or
5 how our neural pathways were changed because we studied piano as children, or how meditation alters our brainwave patterns.

Isolating which part of the brain is responsible for moving your big toe is a neat trick. But what
10 about "softer" functions like figuring out how judgment is formed or music is made? "Why Music Moves Us: The Cognitive Neuroscience[1] of Music," a **conference** at the Swedish Medical Center in Seattle in 2005, tried to ask some
15 **fundamental** questions about how the brain "hears" and translates sound into music.

We know how the ear catches sound and how the sound waves are translated by about 30,000 auditory nerves into electrical and chemical
20 signals that are **transmitted** to the brain. But how is it that the neurons in the brain translate those signals into something we recognize as music? Scans show that the brain is much more actively engaged with music than with speech.
25 But there is no actual **physical** sound in your brain. No notes. No music. Only neurons.

"The idea of pitch is a mental phenomenon," says Robert Zatorre, professor of neuroscience at McGill University in Montreal. Only the way
30 sounds are organized makes them interesting. Brain scans show that different parts of the brain register activity depending on the kind of music played. Dissonance[2], for example, is generally perceived as unpleasant, and it
35 provokes reactions in a different region of the brain than consonant[3] harmonies do.

---

[1] *neuroscience:* the field of science devoted to the study of the nervous system and the brain
[2] *dissonance:* a technical term in music referring to combinations of sounds that are unpleasant together
[3] *consonant:* in music, a term describing notes that sound pleasant together; the opposite of dissonance

Music is a basic human condition. We are born primed to pick up on beat regularities and able to put sound in some sort of coherent order. All cultures have music, and the ability to recognize music comes before speech. The brain is wired with reward and avoidance circuitry, and music rates high in the reward region.

There is strong evidence that our attraction to music isn't just for enjoyment. Music helps build community. Think, for example, of how nations and institutions use songs to bring people together, the thrill of singing your national anthem or the "old school song."

Music can also aid healing. Patients who have suffered strokes or other brain injuries often show dramatic improvement in their recovery if music or rhythm is played during therapy, reported Michael Thaut, professor of music and neuroscience at Colorado State University.

Our understanding of how the brain perceives music is still rudimentary, and researchers haven't even developed reliable tests to measure what we want to know about some of the most basic brain functions. Trying to measure, for example, if the brain has a different electrical reaction to music it likes than to music it doesn't is quite difficult because "like" and "dislike" are subjective terms that are hard to quantify scientifically.

Still, it's clear that our perceptions of the world have a physical **foundation** in the brain, and those perceptions can be altered. Studies have shown, for example, that the recognition of pitch can be altered by as much as 1½ tones with medication.

Mark Tramo, director of the Institute for Music & Brain Science at Harvard Medical School, told the conference that while the field of studying the neuroscience of how we perceive music is still young, someday we'll know enough to be able to plant tiny neuro-bionic chips in the brain to alter perceptions and "fix" problems. It doesn't take much imagination to **project** a little further out and imagine a day when we start to understand how the brain processes ideas or "produces" creativity.

What if it turns out that art and creativity are merely the product of a series of switches in the brain firing off in the right sequence? Would it **diminish** our appreciation of art?

Artists have always occupied a special place in society in part because no one—even artists themselves—has been able to pin down the essential act of making art and explain how inspiration and creativity work. Without a rational explanation for the process of creating art, it's much easier to romanticize[4] the artist and attribute quasi-mystical or religious qualities to artistic ideals.

But what if we are able to eventually reduce creativity to biochemical formulas? Surely that would change the way we look at artists. It might even take the mystery out of their art. If we could create neuro-bionic chips to cure brain disorders, why not pills that induce creativity on demand? If you created under the influence of these pills, would that seem like cheating, somehow? Surely some might claim that neuro-induced art would give some artists unfair advantage over others. Should we care? After all, if good art is really what's important, then who cares how it was created?

And isn't it true that art **incorporates** so much of the artist's experience that even if we are able to unlock biologically-enhanced creativity, it's doubtful that it would result in a surge of "super-art?"

Still, as science gets closer to the intersection of biology and creativity, and the mystery of the artistic impulse is graphed and charted, it's worth pondering what we consider to be the essential qualities that make art unique.

---

4 *romanticize*: make something seem more attractive or interesting than it really is

READING COMPREHENSION

A. Mark each sentence as *T* (true) or *F* (false) according to the information in Reading 1. Use the dictionary to help you understand new words.

.... **1.** Locating the area of the brain that controls toe movement is impossible.

.... **2.** Sound waves themselves do not enter the brain.

.... **3.** People need to learn how to speak before they can appreciate music.

.... **4.** There is evidence that music may help people with brain injuries.

.... **5.** We are now able to improve people's creativity and perception of music with brain implants.

.... **6.** The reading says that neuroscience will destroy our appreciation of art.

.... **7.** The reading implies that artistic success is entirely a product of the physical brain.

.... **8.** The secrets behind artistic success may seem less mysterious in the future.

B. Read these sentences paraphrased from Reading 1. Then, scan the article to find the original sentences. Write the line number of the original on the line.

.... **1.** Listening to music activates the brain more than listening to speech does.

.... **2.** Music is a universal experience for all humans.

.... **3.** The facts suggest that music is for more than just pleasure.

.... **4.** The way we view the world is largely determined by the physical properties of our brains.

.... **5.** We can artificially alter our perception of music.

.... **6.** No doubt we would see artists differently.

READING STRATEGY: Finding the Perpetrator

In this sentence from Reading 1, the subject of the sentence—*researchers*—is the "perpetrator." These *researchers* are doing something.

  Researchers are only now beginning to unlock the secrets of the brain.

When the topic is technical and the style formal, writers often omit mention of the perpetrator. Perhaps the perpetrator is not important, not known, or too obvious.

  Dissonance, for example, is generally perceived as unpleasant.

In this sentence, no perpetrator is indicated, but from the context we know it is "people." We can reword the sentence to show the perpetrator.

  People generally perceive dissonance, for example, as unpleasant.

Read these excerpts from Reading 1. Look at the excerpts in context to determine the perpetrator and then write it in the blank. Write "unknown" if it is not possible to determine the perpetrator from the context.

Excerpt		Perpetrator?
1. ...judgment is formed... (line 11)	*Who or what forms it?*	....
2. ...music is made... (line 11)	*Who or what makes it?*	....
3. We are born primed to pick up on beat regularities... (line 37)	*What primes us?*	....
4. The brain is wired with reward and avoidance circuitry... (line 41)	*Who or what wired it?*	....
5. ...if music or rhythm is played during therapy... (line 53)	*Who or what plays it?*	....
6. ...and those perceptions can be altered. (line 68)	*What can alter them?*	....
7. ...how it was created? (line 108)	*Who created it?*	....
8. ...and the mystery of the artistic impulse is graphed and charted... (line 115)	*Who or what graphed and charted it?*	....

The sentences in the preceding exercise have passive verb forms—*is formed*, *is made*, *can be altered*. With passive verb forms, we can add a prepositional phrase to show the perpetrator. The phrase usually starts with *by* or *with*.

The sound waves are translated <u>by about 30,000 auditory nerves</u> into electrical and chemical signals.

The recognition of pitch can be altered <u>with medication</u>.

"Auditory nerves" and "medication" are the perpetrators.

VOCABULARY ACTIVITIES

Noun	Verb	Adjective	Adverb
conference	confer	....	....
diminishment	diminish	diminishing diminished	....
foundation	....	foundational	....
fundamental	....	fundamental	fundamentally
incorporation	incorporate	incorporated	....
....	....	physical	physically
primacy	prime	prime primed	....
transmission transmitter	transmit	....	....

A. Fill in the blanks with a target word from the chart that completes the sentence in a grammatical and meaningful way. Be sure to use the correct form.

1. Music is .... a product of the brain and its neural mechanisms.

2. The human auditory organs and the brain seem to be .... to respond to music.

3. The scientists held a .... to discuss the latest research into creativity and the brain.

4. The people at the meeting are interested in exploring the neural .... of our appreciation of music.

5. How are the .... properties of sound translated into music that the brain can hear?

6. Neurons .... information via chemical and electrical synapses in the brain.

7. Will our appreciation of art .... if we learn the secrets of human creativity?

8. Art almost certainly .... the artist's personal experiences.

B. Using your dictionary, decide which meaning of the word *physical* is expressed in each sentence. Match it with the definition on the right. Compare answers with a partner.

.... **1.** Pitch is a physical property of sound.

.... **2.** The game became very physical in the 4th quarter.

.... **3.** Ray Harryhausen's stop-motion characters are more physically expressive than puppets.

a. relating to the body

b. relating to natural things that can be observed or measured

c. involving bodily force and contact

The adjective and verb *prime* has several meanings in different contexts.

a. main, most important, most likely, most typical	*prime* example / reason / aim / concern / suspect / target / cause / mover
b. the best, the most perfect or excellent	*prime* position / location / cut (of meat) *prime* time (television)
c. the most productive time	in one's *prime*; past one's *prime*; in the *prime* of life
d. to be prepared or readied	*primed* to learn / to listen / to respond / for action
e. prepare something for use or to get it started	*prime* wood (for painting); *prime* an explosive; *prime* the economy; *prime* someone to take over a job or task

---

C. Which meaning of the word *prime* is expressed in each sentence? Match the sentences with the definitions in the box above. Compare answers with a partner.

.... **1.** We are born primed to pick up on beat regularities and able to put sound in some sort of coherent order.

.... **2.** Prime seats for the show cost over $500 each.

.... **3.** In his final Olympics, he was obviously way past his prime and performed poorly.

.... **4.** Harryhausen's prime concern was to make the figures more realistic and expressive.

.... **5.** To prime the state's economy, the governor cut taxes on businesses and individuals.

Transmit and *transmission* can also be used in several contexts.

a.	send electronically or over airwaves	The broadcast was **transmitted** to over 50 nations.
b.	spread an idea, emotion, or disease	The disease can only be **transmitted** through direct contact.
		He encouraged teachers to **transmit** positive values to their students.
c.	to allow energy to pass through	Water **transmits** sound 4½ times faster than air does.
d.	a piece of machinery in a car	A **transmission** (manual or automatic) **transmits** energy from the car's engine to the axles and wheels.
e.	a radio or TV signal	We listened to the BBC on short-wave radio **transmissions**.

D. Which meaning of *transmit* or *transmission* is expressed in each sentence? Match the sentences with the definitions in the box above. Compare answers with a partner.

.... 1. It came equipped with a 5-speed transmission.

.... 2. An optical fiber permits data in the form of light to be transmitted over long distances.

.... 3. The material absorbs and transmits heat to circulating fluids.

.... 4. The transmission was too weak to be heard.

.... 5. Parents complained that the movie transmitted the wrong values to children.

READING 2

BEFORE YOU READ

Read these questions. Discuss your answers in small groups.

1. Do you know how to play a musical instrument? If so, describe how the instrument produces sound.

2. As a small child in school or at home, did you ever make your own musical instruments out of simple materials—for example, a drum from an old can? Describe what kind of materials you used and what sound the instruments made.

3. If you heard people talking about a Fender, a Martin, a Gibson, a Yamaha, or a Takamine, would you know what subject they were talking about? How about an acoustic or an electric?

MORE WORDS YOU'LL NEED

magnet: an object that attracts other objects toward it, either naturally or because of an electric charge

pluck: to play the strings of a guitar by pulling with the fingers or with a pick

READ

This article describes the guitar's rise to the star musical instrument it is today.

Guitars: The Quest for Volume

Today, people tend to think of the guitar as a loud instrument. Yet, before the 1920s, projecting sound was a problem for the guitar. The volume was simply too low to compete
5 with louder instruments, limiting its use to solo performance and vocal accompaniment. The versatility and portability of the guitar, however, were simply too appealing to allow it to drift into obscurity. Guitar makers began
10 experimenting with new designs and materials that could increase its volume.

To understand the fundamental challenge facing guitar designers, first consider what a guitar is trying to do. A guitar operates on the
15 principle that a tightly stretched string, when plucked, will vibrate rapidly and agitate the air enough to make a musical tone that people can hear. The shorter, tighter, and thinner the string, the more vibrations per second and the higher the
20 pitch of the tone. The longer, looser, and thicker the string, the lower the pitch. So by plucking strings of various thicknesses, tensions, and lengths, a variety of musical notes can be created.

But there's a problem. A vibrating string does
25 not make much sound. It needs to be made louder, or amplified, in some way. Try this grade-school experiment: Wrap a small, thin rubber band around your thumb and index finger. Stretch it tight and pluck it. It will make a sound
30 but not a loud one, and the volume will diminish quickly. Now stretch the rubber band around a small, thin-walled box with one open side. Pluck the string where it crosses the opening. A much louder, longer sound should result. That

35 is because the string vibrates the box, which in turn vibrates the air inside the box and creates a sound. Because the sound can echo a bit, it also sounds fuller—that is, it has a better tone. So, a thin box with an opening makes a rather good
40 amplifier for strings.

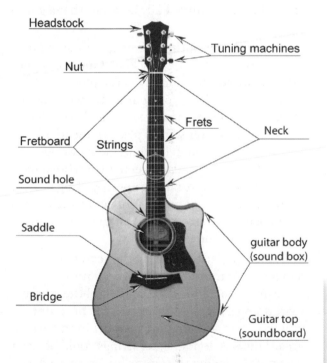

A guitar takes advantage of box amplification by attaching a long piece of wood—the neck—to the hollow guitar body, or sound box. The strings run down the neck to the middle of the
45 body to a piece of wood called the bridge. The bridge has two purposes. It anchors the strings to the guitar top (also called the soundboard). It also contains the saddle, a thin piece of hard material that lifts the strings slightly above the

neck and top. When the strings are plucked, the saddle transmits the vibrations into the guitar body. The wooden sides of the body vibrate the air inside and create an echo that increases the volume of the original vibration. The sound exits through one or more sound holes cut into the top of the guitar.

The shape and dimensions of the guitar body are important in making sure that the vibrations from the different strings are amplified fully and equally. Guitar designers experimented with many different designs. After much **refinement**, they found that a figure-eight shape with a larger and a smaller chamber separated by a narrower waist works best. This shape best amplifies and smoothes the sound of all the tones that a guitar can make.

Even with this optimal design, a guitar made entirely of wood is not very loud. Guitar designers faced an **intrinsic** difficulty in the physical properties and design of a guitar. Heavier, tighter strings are louder. Thinner wood is also louder. But heavier, tighter strings place tremendous **stress** on the guitar, requiring thicker wood to strengthen the guitar and keep it from breaking. So the increase in volume gained by using heavier strings and greater tension is offset by the thicker wood needed to strengthen the guitar. Guitars, it seemed, would never be loud.

In the early 20th century, the search for a louder guitar intensified. Two solutions appeared. One design strengthened the guitar by running a metal rod through the neck of the guitar and by adding more support in the bridge area. This way, louder steel strings could be used without damaging the guitar. Today, these design improvements are incorporated into most hollow body, steel-string guitars. The second solution added metal resonator plates[1] to the top of the guitar to take advantage of the "twangy" acoustic properties of metal. The twang not only made guitars louder, but the change in tone helped them stand out more when played along with other instruments.

With these modifications and added features, guitars could be heard more easily, but they still could not fill a large building with sound. Here is where advances in electronics play a role. One possibility, of course, is to put a microphone in front of the guitar. In **theory**, this works well enough. In practice, it can create several problems. The microphone limits a player's movements, and it often picks up other sounds, amplifying them along with the sound of the guitar. Even when everything works perfectly, the core problem remains: the guitar itself is not any louder.

Achieving a true electric guitar required a complete rethinking of how a guitar could work. Rather than have the guitar body amplify the sound, the body would merely be a platform that holds vibrating strings—similar to those on an acoustic guitar—and electronics. The body could even be solid, not hollow. With a solid body, the strings make a very soft sound—softer than the sound achieved in the rubber-band-around-the-box experiment, and not nearly enough to amplify successfully through a typical microphone. Instead of a hollow sound box, the strings are placed just above tiny magnets, or pickups. When the strings vibrate, they create a weak, but precise disturbance in the pickup's magnetic field[2]. That disturbance (the audio signal) is transmitted as a weak electrical current through wires and cables to an electrical device that amplifies the signal through a speaker, sometimes to ear-splitting levels. By the 1950s, electrics were revolutionizing popular music.

Meanwhile, efforts were being made to electrify what were now called acoustic guitars—the steel string guitar made of wood. Amplification is achieved by placing pickups inside the guitar body. These pickups contain a mechanism (a piezo-electric transducer)

[1] *resonator plate*: a device, typically a metal plate, for making sound loud and clear
[2] *magnetic field*: the area around a magnet influenced by the positive and negative poles

that is sensitive to vibration. They transmit an electrical version of the vibration through wires to an amplifier. The thinking here is that by capturing body vibration, the amplified sound will have a more natural tone, and it does. There are many competing designs, and the technology is constantly changing, but whatever their form, internal pickups allow traditional acoustic guitars to achieve greater amplification while maintaining the acoustic guitar sound.

Electronic amplification opened the door for musicians to experiment with sound in other ways. Before sound can be amplified electronically, it must be converted into an electronic signal, and this signal can be modified to achieve different effects. Think of it this way: the volume and tone of an acoustic guitar are mainly the result of its materials and design. A well-designed acoustic guitar made of good materials sounds better than a less carefully constructed one. With a solid body electric guitar, however, the electronics build and shape the instrument's naturally thin tone by enriching the audio signal before it is transmitted to speakers.

After decades of research and development, guitar players can now **manipulate** and modify the audio signal in the most astounding ways. Just consider the colorful vocabulary they use to describe the sounds of an electric guitar—crunch, punch, fuzz, flange, wah wah, chorus, screaming, delay, gated. Some of the possibilities are quite unpleasant. Others add to the library of wonderful sounds that are used to make music. These acoustic gifts are the unexpected but natural consequence of the long effort to do one simple thing—to make a very mellow instrument a little bit, or a whole lot, louder.

READING COMPREHENSION

Mark each statement as *A* (referring to the acoustic guitar), *E* (solid body electric guitar), or *B* (both) according to the information in Reading 2.

.... **1.** The shape of the guitar has only a marginal effect on the sound.

.... **2.** String thickness and tightness determine the pitch of a note.

.... **3.** This guitar cannot be used in a live performance with a large audience without electronic help.

.... **4.** Thinner material in the guitar body improves the volume of the instrument.

.... **5.** Capturing the sound electronically requires a device that senses vibrating air or vibrating materials inside the guitar.

.... **6.** This guitar cannot be played through a microphone.

.... **7.** This guitar works on the principle that a vibrating string creates a disturbance.

.... **8.** The bridge and saddle transmit vibration to the guitar body, which amplifies the sound.

READING STRATEGY: Point of View

A technical process or design can be described from several points of view depending on the purpose and audience. Here is a simple electric guitar setup involving three components connected by cables.

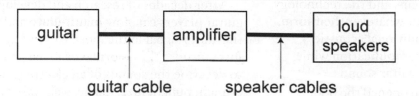

Read these paragraphs describing the diagram above from different points of view. For each paragraph, complete the task.

Description

1. How do I set it up?

Insert one end of a guitar cable into the jack in the electric guitar. Insert the other end of the cable into the input jack on the amplifier. Then run speaker cables from the output jacks of the amplifier to the input terminals of the speakers.

2. How is it set up or designed?

One end of a guitar cable is inserted into the jack in the guitar. The other end is plugged into the input jack in the amplifier. A speaker cable runs from the output jack of the amplifier to the input jack of the loud speaker.

3. How does it work?

When the guitarist plucks a string, the guitar sends a weak electric signal through a cable to an amplifier. The amplifier increases the energy in the signal and transmits this stronger signal via cables to loud speakers. The speakers turn the signal back into sound.

4. What happens to the signal?

When a guitar string is plucked, a weak electrical signal is transmitted through a cable to an amplifier, a device that adds energy to the signal. This amplified signal is delivered through speaker cables to loud speakers where the signal is converted back into sound.

Task

This version gives instructions to the reader. Underline the verbs that tell the reader what to do.

This version describes the setup without indicating who set it up. Underline any intransitive verbs. (See Unit 3, page 45, for more on transitive and intransitive verbs.)

This version tells what each device does. The verbs are active—*plucks*, *sends*, *increases*. Underline the "perpetrators" of the action described by each active verb.

This version tells what happens to the sound signal. The passive verbs make the paragraph seem technical or scientific. Underline the passive verbs.

VOCABULARY ACTIVITIES

Noun	Verb	Adjective	Adverb
....	....	intrinsic	intrinsically
manipulation	manipulate	manipulative	manipulatively
projectile* projection	project	projected	....
refinement	refine	refined	....
stress	stress	stressful stressed	stressfully
theory	theorize	theoretical	theoretically

*The noun *project* will be treated in Unit 9.

A. Fill in the blanks with a target word from the chart that completes the sentence in a grammatical and meaningful way. Be sure to use the correct form.

1. Although it is .... possible for a guitar to be made of a single wood, most guitars use a variety of woods.

2. Wood is a popular material for guitars because it can be .... in many ways, including shaping, bowing, and slicing.

3. Woods are selected for their ability to impart sound, their beauty when finished, and their ability to withstand the .... of day-to-day playing.

4. Several approaches are available for .... sound in large spaces.

5. The technology for amplifying acoustic guitars is still being ....

B. In the reading, *stress* refers to physical force, but it can also refer to emphasis or to psychological pressure. In your notebook, write sentences that link these words in a meaningful and grammatical way. Compare sentences with a partner.

1. consultant / stress / need / better quality control
   The consultant stressed the need for better quality control.
2. teacher / stress / read Chapter 5 very carefully
3. assign / too many tasks at once / stressful
4. must / greater stress on / open / new markets for our products
5. psychologist / stress / multitasking / not a reliable strategy for saving time
6. feel stress / work / go to school / at the same time

C. Discuss these questions in a small group; then write a paragraph for each about your ideas. Be prepared to read aloud and discuss your paragraphs in class.

1. What are some good ways to relieve stress when a busy schedule leaves little time for rest and recreation?

2. What skills or courses should high schools stress the most?

D. Like the word *stress*, the verbs *project* and *manipulate* can have physical and psychological senses. Match the meaning of the word in each sentence with the most appropriate definition on the left.

Project

.... 1. The company projected a 4% increase in sales.

.... 2. The 3-D image is projected onto a screen with angled ridges.

.... 3. The actor's voice projects well.

.... 4. She projects the image of confident leadership.

.... 5. He projected his own fears about succeeding in college onto his friends.

.... 6. Several stock market analysts projected record earnings this year.

a. estimate future quantities / sizes / amounts

b. make an image or sound fill a space

c. give an impression to other people

d. assume that others have the same thoughts or feelings

Manipulate

.... 1. They all grew tired of their boss's manipulative behavior.

.... 2. She learned to manipulate the clumsy machine.

.... 3. The computer can manipulate huge amounts of data.

.... 4. The lawyer tried to manipulate the jury by playing on their emotions.

.... 5. The teacher sensed that her students were trying to manipulate her.

.... 6. The manipulative child convinced his mother that buying him the toy would make *her* happy.

a. operate or manage something skillfully

b. process data/information smoothly

c. use or control people in a tricky, dishonest way

d. good at controlling people in a tricky way

Collocations Chart

Verb/Adverb	Adjective	Noun
confer	....	greatness, an advantage, titles, prizes, rewards (on sb)
rapidly, gradually	*diminishing* *diminished*	resources, role, prospects, expectations, returns, number, effect, threat
....	*fundamental*	change, questions, issues, difference, principle, shift, problem, concept
learn, grasp, teach, master, cover, explain	basic	*fundamentals*
....	*intrinsic*	value, motivation, part, limitation, problem, flaw, sense, rewards, nature, reason
highly, very, more, less, increasingly, continuously, gradually	*refined*	....
advance, have, confirm, prove, disprove, support, test, challenge, propose	complete, new, current	*theory* (that…) *theory* (of…)

E. The chart above shows some common collocations, or word partners, for selected target vocabulary. Refer to the chart and complete these sentences. Compare work with a partner.

1. Drawing on several studies, some child development specialists have proposed a .... that listening to Mozart's music may .... several advantages on children, calming them and helping them think spatially.

2. Other researchers feel they have uncovered .... flaws in the studies and doubt that briefly listening to Mozart before attempting a task has any significant effect.

3. They warn that the "Mozart Effect" is a rapidly .... one. In fact, any mental stimulation before doing a task showed a similar effect.

4. By the age of six, Mozart had mastered the .... of keyboard instruments and the violin. Already a composer, he began touring and giving concerts.

5. The clavichord, a stringed keyboard, sounds beautiful but has one .... limitation—its lack of volume means it cannot be heard well when other instruments are playing.

continued

6. By the 18th century, violin-making had become highly ……………refined……………, and violins from that era still set the standards for violin perfection.

7. Several ……………fundamental…………… changes were made to violins in this era, most noticeably in the length and angle of the neck.

WRITING AND DISCUSSION TOPICS

1. The "Mozart Effect" refers to the claim that briefly listening to Mozart before taking a test can improve test scores. Do some research on the "Mozart Effect" and write a paragraph explaining what you found.

2. Do you feel that music education is important? In other words, should the study of music be a part of every child's education?

3. Worldwide, the violin and piano may be the main instruments children are taught to play in structured settings where they can receive formal instruction. But guitars are often the instrument people choose when they want to play for fun. What makes the guitar so appealing?

4. We humans seem to love music, but we do not seem to love the same music. What factors influence individuals to prefer a certain kind of music?

5. Here is a diagram showing a simple setup for a guitar and microphone. Do one or more of the following:

   • Give instructions on how to set up the system.

   • Describe the components in the system and how they are connected.

   • Describe what happens to the sound from the microphone and electric guitar.

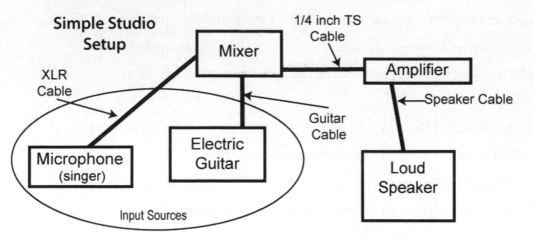

This setup allows two sources of input—a microphone for singing and a guitar for musical accompaniment. It has four types of cables. The mixer is a device that combines the voice and guitar so that they can be sent together to the amplifier and loud speaker.

SENSORY PERCEPTION

In this unit, you will

- ➲ read about how the mind perceives odors and musical notes.
- ➲ practice categorizing information using charts and graphs.
- ➲ increase your understanding of the target academic words for this unit:

category	dimension	likewise	philosophy	stable
concurrent	entity	minimum	plus	unify
cycle	identical	parameter	principal	

SELF-ASSESSMENT OF TARGET WORDS

Think carefully about how well you know each target word in this unit. Then, write it in the appropriate column in the chart. When you've finished this unit, come back and reassess your knowledge of the target words.

I have never seen the word before.	I have seen the word but am not sure what it means.	I understand the word when I see or hear it in a sentence.	I have tried to use the word, but I am not sure I am using it correctly.	I use the word with confidence in either speaking or writing.	I use the word with confidence, both in speaking and writing.

BEFORE YOU READ

Read these questions. Discuss your answers in small groups.

1. Does adding smell to movies and video games strike you as a useful improvement? What technical challenges would adding smell likely involve?

2. What other uses can you see for a machine that could reproduce odors? In businesses? In the home?

3. Odors can often trigger powerful memories. For example, the smell of bread baking may remind someone of their childhood home. What memories do you associate with certain odors?

MORE WORDS YOU'LL NEED

simulate: to create an effect or situation that seems real but actually is not

olfactory: connected with smell—*olfactory* nerves / cells / neurons / sense

nontoxic: not poisonous; safe to eat, breathe, or touch

READ

This article discusses why, unlike sound, it is so difficult to add smell to movies.

Virtual Odors?

Movies have successfully captured sights and sounds on film since the 1920s. And today we can enjoy realistic and imaginary multimedia delights even on hand-held devices.
5 But if such treats for the eye and ear are now commonplace, why is there no machine that can readily incorporate our sense of smell into the experience of a movie or a video game?

Actually, movie makers have tried to add
10 this missing **dimension**. In 1959, a film called *Behind the Great Wall* piped odors through the air-conditioning system of a theater. The 1960 film *Scent of a Mystery*, featuring Smell-O-Vision, opened in a theater equipped to release
15 smells in synch with the movie. Director John Waters gave "scratch-and-sniff" cards out to accompany his "Odorama" movie *Polyester* (1982). And Walt Disney World's Epcot theme park near Orlando, Florida uses odors
20 to enhance its *Journey into the Imagination* attraction. So far, though, Smell-O-Vision-type devices are no more than gimmicks of only marginal interest. Why? No affordable machine can store enough odors to simulate more than a
25 small fraction of what humans can smell.

Sound and color simulation do not face such limitations. Computer monitors, for example, can recreate millions of colors because it really only takes three colors to do so. A screen that
30 can display tiny red, green, and blue pixels[1] can combine these colors to reproduce most colors that a human eye can see. Sound waves, though quite complex, can be defined mathematically, reproduced by a synthesizer[2] and amplified
35 electronically.

Odors are different. They cannot be manipulated or defined mathematically.

---

[1] *pixels*: minute areas of light on a computer screen, which together form an image
[2] *synthesizer*: a machine that produces different sounds electronically

As Jaron Lanier explains in an article in *New Scientist*, odors "are not patterns of energy, like images or sounds. To smell an apple, you breathe hundreds or thousands of apple molecules into your nose." There is no way to amplify them other than adding more such molecules. **Plus**, each molecule that triggers smell is unique. This means a machine cannot produce all possible odors by simply mixing three odors. It is true that odor-causing chemicals can be combined to produce millions of scents, but the **minimum** number of basic odors required would be in the many hundreds, perhaps thousands, to simulate all the scents that humans can sense.

Several odor **parameters** can be identified that might be useful. We can talk about the intensity of an odor or the persistence of an odor. We can label it as pleasant or unpleasant. Non-offensive odors can be grouped into seven general **categories**: medicinal, floral, chemical, fruity, vegetable, fishy, and earthy. They can also be categorized by how they feel in our nose: tingly, burning, warm, metallic, pungent, itching, sharp, and cool. But there are simply too many odors in each category to design a practical device that could reference and recreate all the scents we can smell. Jaron Lanier says, "Colors and sounds can be measured with rulers, but odors must be looked up in a dictionary."

That dictionary is in the brain. Odors are detected deep in the nasal passage when molecules come into contact with the olfactory epithelium—a patch of tissue covered with neurons. These neurons have receptors[3] that can detect a particular molecule. If a molecule fits into a matching receptor, the brain gets a signal. Apparently, the human nose has about one thousand different types of olfactory neurons.

The brain's "smell dictionary" categorizes odors but not in a way that a chemistry book would. Instead the brain groups smells according to what they mean in the real world. Things that emit a rotting smell, for example, get very special handling. Interpreting smell also requires help from the other senses, and its meaning may derive from the context. Whether a smell is good or bad may depend on where you smell it and what you think is causing it. If a bowl of ice cream smells like hard-boiled eggs, you probably won't eat it even if you like hard-boiled eggs. In other words, smells function a bit like words do. We know thousands of different words, and the meaning of a word depends on the context in which it occurs. We define a word by pointing to the **entity** it refers to or by comparing its meaning to other words. With scents, we may say "it smells like a cucumber" or "it has a soapy smell."

If millions of visible colors can be produced from just three primary colors, is there any hope of finding smell "pixels" that will trigger the perception of smell in our brains? We, of course, see images on computer screens that look real to us even though the objects are not really there. They are optical illusions. **Likewise**, sound recordings and even your cell phone create an auditory illusion—the source of the original sound only seems to be present. Is it possible to design a mechanism that could somehow manipulate our brain to create the illusion of smell when no odor molecules are present— virtual odors?

In the near future, this achievement seems remote, but some progress is being made in research on machines that can mimic the sense of smell. These "electric noses" are equipped with olfactory sensors that detect specific odors. In order to design such a machine, scientists and engineers must be able to classify and identify an odor's distinctive "fingerprint" and design a mechanism that can electronically detect that fingerprint. The possible value of such a machine in food inspection, medicine, and law enforcement has prompted several dozen companies to develop and sell electronic nose units.

---

[3] *receptor*: a cell or device that reacts to changes such as temperature, light, or sound

If a machine can digitally detect odors, perhaps the reverse is possible. The Tokyo Institute of Technology is reported to be working on an odor recorder and generator. The plan is to design a gadget that can be pointed at an object, record its odor through 15 electronic noses, and recreate the odor by mixing together and vaporizing odors from a set of 96 nontoxic chemicals. If this device succeeds, it will move well beyond current odor generators. These emit only a small number of odors and have failed commercially.

If odor recorders and generators prove to be feasible and affordable, Smell-o-Vision may be primed for a comeback, adding a new dimension to the movie going experience. It may even require a new film rating system: "Warning: This movie is rated R for Rotten. Contains odors that some may find offensive."

READING COMPREHENSION

Mark each sentence as *T* (true) or *F* (false) according to the information in Reading 1. Use the dictionary to help you understand new words.

.... 1. A machine that can synthesize most smells would already exist if there were a market for it.

.... 2. At the present, the entertainment industry is using smell in limited ways.

.... 3. Virtually all colors that humans can see can be synthesized.

.... 4. Odors, like sounds, are created by energy waves coming from foods and other substances.

.... 5. A pleasurable smell will always remain so no matter where it occurs.

.... 6. At this time, electronic nose technology has more obvious practical applications than a smell generator does.

READING STRATEGY: Categorizing

When we group entities into categories that do not overlap, we say the categories are *mutually exclusive*. For example, musical instruments used in orchestras fall into mutually exclusive categories. There are wind instruments, string instruments, and percussion instruments.

A. These sentences are based on the readings in Units 4 and 5. For each sentence, answer the questions shown in the example. Write "not sure" if information is missing.

1. Guitars can be classified into acoustic and electric guitars.

What entities are being categorized?	Guitars.
What is the basis for the categorization?	The way the sound is amplified.
Are the categories mutually exclusive?	No. Some guitars are both acoustic and electric.

2. There are two types of acoustic guitars—steel-stringed and nylon-stringed.

3. Non-offensive odors can be grouped into seven general categories: medicinal, floral, chemical, fruity, vegetable, fishy, and earthy.

4. Odors can also be classified by the way they feel in our nose: tingly, burning, warm, metallic, pungent, itching, sharp, and cool.

5. We can label odors as pleasant or unpleasant.

> Categorizing may require us to draw a "dividing line" in order to create categories. Reading 1, for example, says odors can be identified by their intensity or their persistence. These two dimensions involve measurements for which there are many possibilities.

B. Examine these categories. Where would you draw the line? Why?

1. childhood and adulthood
2. middle age and old age
3. a short film and a feature film
4. a luxury car and other cars
5. the modern era and the "old days"
6. the poverty line (poor vs. non-poor)

C. This chart categorizes odors along two dimensions: how they smell and how they feel in the nose. Think of one item for each description square. A banana, for example, could be categorized as smelling *fruity* and feeling *warm*.

		tingly	burning	warm	metallic	pungent	itching	sharp	cool
	How odors feel in the nose								
How odors smell	medicinal								
	floral								
	chemical								
	fruity			banana					
	vegetable								
	fishy								
	earthy								

VOCABULARY ACTIVITIES

Noun	Verb	Adjective	Adverb/Conjunction
category categorization	categorize	categorized categorical	categorically
dimension	....	dimensional	dimensionally
entity	....	....	....
....	....	....	likewise
minimum	minimize	minimum/minimal	minimally
parameter	....	....	....
....	....	....	plus

A. Fill in the blanks with a target word from the chart that completes the sentence in a grammatical and meaningful way. Be sure to use the correct form.

1. Guitars can be .... as either electric or acoustic.

2. Most people consider special effects to be part of the movie business, not a separate ....

3. What's the .... number of colors you can use and still have good image on the computer screen?

4. A standard movie screen provides a two-............................. viewing experience.

5. Even a .... amount of black paint will make white paint gray.

6. Coffee falls into the .... of bitter tastes, as opposed to sweet, salty, or sour.

7. Odors would add a whole new .... to the movie-going experience.

B. The word *likewise* signals that the writer is giving another similar, but not identical, case. The word *plus* adds one more piece of supporting information. Fill in the blanks with *likewise* or *plus*. Compare answers with a partner.

1. The original 3-D movies ran into problems. It was difficult to keep the two projectors in sync. The glasses distorted color and caused headaches. .... , the effect did not work well throughout the entire theater.

2. With auditory perception, technically speaking, no sound gets past the ear. The sound waves are converted to a signal that is sent to the brain. .... , the human eye absorbs various wavelengths of light and sends information about that light to the brain.

3. The microphone limits a player's movements, and it often picks up other sounds, amplifying them along with the sound of the guitar. .... , it still does not make the guitar itself any louder.

4. The treatment is completely free, even for people who have no health insurance. .... , it has no side effects.

The reading contains three very abstract nouns: *dimension*, *entity*, and *parameter*. Entity can refer to anything that can be identified as having a separate and independent existence.

> *A corporation is a legal **entity**.*
>
> *The Congress of the United States is a political **entity**.*
>
> *Since the two banks merged, First Bank no longer exists as a separate **entity**.*

Dimension can refer to the physical size and measurements of something. It can also refer to different aspects of things, like the different *dimensions* of a problem or new *dimensions* of sound technology. The word *dimensional* is used to describe space as *two-dimensional* (flat) or *three-dimensional*, as in a 3-D movie.

> *The **dimensions** of the room are 10 × 12 feet.*
>
> *Smell would add a new **dimension** to virtual reality games.*
>
> *The **dimensions** of the problems they face are huge.*
>
> *Humans inhabit **three-dimensional** space.*
>
> *Some people say that time is the fourth **dimension**.*

Parameter is mainly used in academic and technical discussions in fields such as statistics, computer science, mathematics, and engineering. In more common usage, it may refer to agreed upon boundaries or limits for a particular activity.

> *The committee set the **parameters** for awarding scholarships.*
>
> *Exploring the toxicity of these odors is outside the **parameters** of this study.*

C. Fill in the blanks with *entity*, *dimension*, or *parameter*. Use plural forms when necessary.

1. By 1856, the Whig Party no longer existed as a functioning political ....

2. The birth of their first child added a new .... to their lives.

3. The committee, after a lengthy discussion, agreed to work within the .... that they had established earlier that year.

4. In "hyperdrive," the starship enters a separate .... where the speed of light is much faster and the distances between objects much less.

continued

5. The business was penalized for working outside the .... set up by the government.

6. After the hurricane, the city began a cleanup and rebuilding effort of staggering ....

7. Before the reorganization, the two departments operated as separate ....

READING 2

BEFORE YOU READ

Read these questions. Discuss your answers in small groups.

1. A standard riddle of popular philosophy is this question: If a tree falls in a forest and there is nobody to hear it, does it make a sound? What do you think? To answer this question, start by discussing what is meant by the term "sound."

2. *Onomatopoeic* words imitate the sounds they describe. Here is a list of onomatopoeic words in English. What entity (object, force, or animal) do you think might be associated with each sound?

bang	ding dong	splash ....
caw	peep	tick ....
chirp	pop	thump ....
clang	quack	wheeze ....
click	roar	whirr ....
clunk	rumble	whoosh ....
crack	rustle	woof ....
crunch	slurp	zip ....

MORE WORDS YOU'LL NEED

fluctuations: repeated increases and decreases in something

flux: a state of constant change

eardrum: a membrane in the ear that is sensitive to air vibration. A membrane is a thin piece of tissue.

This article explains how sound is perceived as musical notes in the brain.

Pitch and Timbre

One **unifying** characteristic of human life is music. In fact, no known human culture lacks music. But what is there about human perception that allows us to hear sound as
5 musical notes? Why do instruments playing an **identical** note sound different?

The answer to these questions requires some insight into how humans perceive pitch. When a musical instrument is played properly, it vibrates
10 in a predictable way and pushes on the air in and around the instrument. This action creates waves or pulses that travel through the air. You might think of these waves as brief fluctuations in air pressure. Pitch relates to how close
15 together these waves or pulses are. If the musical instrument vibrates 120 times a second, about the same as a typical adult male speaking voice, we say the sound has a frequency of 120 **cycles** per second, or in current terminology 120 Hz
20 (pronounced Hertz, the name of a 19th century German physicist). The typical female speaking voice has a vibration frequency of around 220 Hz. Notes with a low frequency of vibration are referred to as low notes and those with a high
25 frequency as high notes.

Pitch is tied to the vibration of air, but it is ultimately a product of how our ear and brain interpret these vibrations. Vibrating air molecules push against our eardrums, causing
30 them to vibrate at the same frequency. The vibration is then amplified by mechanisms in the middle ear. The amplified vibration stimulates nerve sensors that convert the vibrations into electrical signals that the brain can analyze.
35 What we perceive as pitch is a mental image of those vibrations. Although the vibrating air molecules are quite real, pitch occurs only in the brain. So we may need to reconsider the **philosophical** question "If a tree falls in a forest
40 and nobody is present to hear it, does it make a sound?" The air vibrates, of course, but can there be a sound without eardrums present to vibrate and a brain to interpret the vibrations?

The human ear and brain have limits and
45 cannot assign a pitch to all frequencies of vibration. We cannot hear sounds below 20 Hz or so, and if a sound is below 30–35 Hz, we do not perceive it as a distinct musical note. It sounds toneless, like a rumble. The same is
50 true at the high end. Human hearing tops out at about 20,000 Hz even though air can vibrate at frequencies many times higher. As with the very low frequencies, frequencies above about 4,000 Hz do not sound like musical notes. They begin
55 to sound like snaps, hisses, clicks, and squeaks. You can test this aspect of human perception by playing the very lowest and highest notes on the 88-key piano. To most people, they seem a little musically "off" or lifeless.

60 The brain does interesting things with the arithmetic of pitch. If an instrument plays a note with a frequency of 220 Hz and another one at twice as many cycles per second at 440 Hz, we hear the same musical note (both an A in the C
65 major scale). We say they are an octave[1] apart. Likewise we hear an A if the frequency doubles again and vibrates at 880, 1760, and 3,520 Hz. At the lower end, we hear an A note at 110 Hz and 55 Hz. All told, we can hear between 7 and 8
70 octaves. Outside these ranges the notes become indistinct.

The fascinating arithmetic of musical notes allows the brain to play a trick on us that helps us distinguish sounds. Due to the physics of
75 sound and the materials that make sound, there is no such thing as a pure tone. We may think a note is pure, but we are hearing much more. If a piano plays an A note with a frequency of 110 Hz, it actually plays a note at that frequency plus
80 all the whole number multiples above it—220 (2 × 110), 330 (3 × 110), 440 (4 × 110), 550, 660,

---

[1] *octave*: the distance between the highest and lowest notes on an eight-note scale

and so forth. The loudest frequency, the one with the most energy, is usually the lowest frequency (in this case 110 Hz). It is called
85 the fundamental frequency, the frequency we identify as the pitch of the note. The higher frequencies are called overtones, or harmonics. You hear only one note, rather than dozens of evenly spaced notes, but that is because your
90 brain works behind the scenes and uses the harmonics for other purposes.

You can experiment with harmonics using a guitar (or any string instrument). Pluck the thickest string on the guitar. If your guitar uses
95 standard tuning, you will hear an E (about 82.4 Hz). Now very lightly rest your finger against the string at its exact midpoint (the 12th fret). Pluck the string again and you will hear a softer, rather pretty-sounding E note one octave
100 higher. By lightly touching the string, your finger has absorbed the vibration produced by the fundamental frequency before it could reach the guitar body and be amplified. What's left are the higher harmonics.

105 Overtones and harmonics are also involved in shaping a musical instrument's tone or sound quality—its timbre (pronounced TAM-ber or TIM-ber). Timbre is the **principal** feature of sound we use to recognize each other's voices
110 or distinguish a dog's bark from a baby's cry. With musical instruments, timbre is partly determined by the way an instrument amplifies or dampens harmonics. A trumpet, for example, which is made of brass, amplifies the harmonics
115 rather evenly. A clarinet, because it is shaped differently and made of different materials, amplifies some harmonics more than others.

You can see the effect that an instrument's shape has on tone by considering what your
120 mouth does when you make vowel sounds. If you sing the words "tea" and "too" and use the same musical note, the fundamental frequency is the same for both words. But "tea" sounds different because you changed the shape of your mouth in

125 such a way as to dampen the overtones between about 500 Hz and 2,000 Hz. To make the vowel in the word "too," your mouth amplifies the overtones between 500 and 1,000 Hz and dampens the higher ones. Confusing, for sure,
130 but your brain is hard-wired[2] to handle such calculations automatically and adjust for the different fundamental frequencies of high and low voices.

Timbre is determined by more than just the
135 loudness of overtones. All musical instruments make sounds when a musician commits some sort of controlled violence against the device. We strike keys, blow horns, pluck strings, scrape violins with a bow, beat drums. These
140 actions all make noises that occur before a note can sound. This initial burst of sound, called the attack, is not particularly musical. It is the sound of clicks as keys are hit, hollow thumps as fingers cover holes, the friction of fingers
145 rubbing against strings, hissing before a horn has enough energy to vibrate, tongues tapping and pulling away from mouthpieces. After the attack phase, there is a more **stable** phase when the note's fundamental frequency and overtone
150 patterns emerge. Experiments show that if the attack phase is removed from a recording of an instrument, people have trouble identifying the instrument. Clearly, the way an instrument moves into a note is part of its distinctive sound.

155 The final dimension of timber is the instrument's flux. Flux refers to the fluctuations that occur throughout the duration of a note, such as slight variations in pitch and volume. A trumpet, like many wind instruments, has
160 very little flux. Its tone is fairly stable as the note proceeds. Percussive instruments tend to have a lot of flux. Think of the sound of a large gong struck with a lot of force. Its sound alters significantly as the gong returns to its
165 nonvibrating state.

Other dimensions of sound contribute to a musical instrument's character—its volume, the

---

[2] *hard-wired*: computer terminology, a function that does not require software; here, something the brain does quickly and automatically without conscious learning

duration of its notes, the speed at which it can be played, its register (the lowest and highest notes it can play), and the number of notes it can play **concurrently**. The workings of these elements may seem more intuitively obvious than the puzzling physics of pitch and timbre.

But they too contribute to what we perceive as music by taking advantage of the way our brains process the subtle vibration patterns of air molecules. In the end, the only place these instruments make music is in our heads.

READING COMPREHENSION

Mark each sentence as *T* (true) or *F* (false) according to the information in Reading 2. Use the dictionary to help you understand new words.

.... **1.** Humans are able to hear only a fraction of the possible frequencies of air vibration.

.... **2.** The piano covers the whole range of sound that humans can hear.

.... **3.** The number of octaves we can hear is only limited by the range of frequencies we can hear.

.... **4.** The reading suggests that music and human language take advantage of some of the same properties of sound.

.... **5.** A trumpet is an example of a percussive instrument.

.... **6.** Musical instruments vary in how many notes they can play simultaneously.

READING STRATEGY: Interpreting Charts, Tables, and Graphs

A. This chart lists frequencies of sound discussed in Reading 2. Match the label on the right to the frequency indicated.

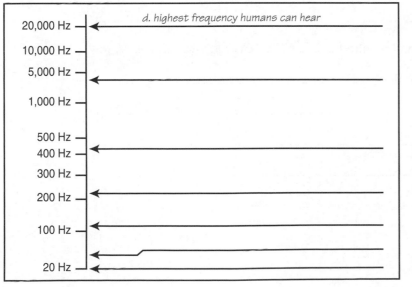

Labels
a. a man's speaking voice
b. a woman's speaking voice
c. the musical note A
d. highest frequency humans can hear
e. the lowest musical note
f. the lowest frequency humans can hear
g. the highest musical note

Academic readings often include tables and charts to report data and statistics. When the numbers in a table are large and end with one or more zeroes, they are usually not exact figures. They are approximate or rounded. In this case, some tables leave out the zeroes and indicate how many zeroes are missing by saying "in thousands" or "in millions" beneath the table title. When reporting data or statistics, be sure to add the missing zeroes back to the number.

iPod Sales	
Year	iPods Sold
2002	376,000
2003	937,000
2004	4,416,000
2005	22,497,000
2006	39,409,000
Total	67,635,000

iPod Sales (in thousands)	
Year	iPods Sold
2002	376
2003	937
2004	4,416
2005	22,497
2006	39,409
Total	67,635

Source: Apple Inc.

B. Complete these sentences based on the information in the tables above. Be sure to add back any missing zeroes. Then, write three more sentences giving more information from the tables. Use the sentence patterns from items 1 to 6 in your sentences.

1. In 2003, Apple sold .... iPods.

2. In 2004, there were .... iPods sold.

3. Between 2003 and 2004, iPod sales increased by ....

4. In 2005, iPod sales reached ....

5. By the end of 2006, Apple sales had reached ....

6. From 2002 to 2006, iPod sales totaled ....

7. ....

8. ....

9. ....

VOCABULARY ACTIVITIES

Noun	Verb	Adjective	Adverb
....	....	concurrent	concurrently
cycle	cycle recycle	cyclical	cyclically
....	....	identical	identically
philosophy philosopher	philosophize	philosophical	philosophically
principal	....	principal	principally
stability	stabilize	stable	....
unity unification	unify	unified unifying	....

A. Fill in the blank with a target word from the box that completes the sentence in a grammatical and meaningful way. Be sure to use the correct form.

> cycle   identical   stable
> concurrent   principal

One curious auditory phenomenon is the ability of many humans to hear a missing fundamental frequency. Sound waves are vibrations of air, measured in

(1) .... per second. A musical note is a particularly

(2) .... sound that always sends out the same number of vibrations per second. In reality, though, a musical note sends out several different sound waves

(3) .... The one with the lowest frequency is called the fundamental frequency. It is also the loudest. The other sound waves are called overtones. Curiously, their frequencies of vibration are exact multiples of the fundamental frequency. Middle C on the piano, for example, has a fundamental frequency of 261.63. But it sends out a weaker sound wave that vibrates approximately 523 times per second, another at 785, another at 1047, and so on.

Since the fundamental frequency is the loudest tone, shouldn't it be the

(4) .... component that we use to identify the pitch of a note? Maybe not. If we remove the fundamental frequency from a sound recording, many people still hear a note at the (5) .... pitch. Our brain apparently measures the intervals between the overtones and figures out the original note. Due to this phenomenon, a small loud speaker, such as in a telephone, can create the

continued

illusion that it is broadcasting a lower note than it is actually capable of producing. Deep voices still seem deep.

Can you hear missing fundamentals? Recent evidence from German researchers suggests that humans vary in what note they hear by as much as four octaves. Typing "missing fundamental" in a search engine will lead you to sites where you can test what you hear.

B. Circle the word or phrase that best captures the meaning of the target word in each sentence.

1. The coach was **philosophical** about the team's disappointing defeat.
   a. stoical and calm   **b.** theoretical
2. Many of the bank's customers were nervous about risking their **principal**.
   a. money invested   **b.** the school director
3. It takes about 30 minutes to complete the exercise **cycle**.
   a. bicycle   **b.** a sequence of exercises
4. The patient's condition was **stable** after the surgery.
   a. not getting worse   **b.** improving
5. They **cycled** around the town for several hours.
   a. rode their bikes   **b.** rode around the same route
6. Their plan was **identical to** the one they used last time.
   a. similar to   **b.** the same as

C. Build sentences using a random generator: Your teacher or partner calls out a random two-digit number to identify two words from the lists below. You then use those words to write a grammatical and meaningful sentence.

Teacher: "2-1." [The two words are "identical" (2) and "cycle" (1).]

Possible sentence: "The two species have nearly identical life cycles."

0. philosophical	0. concurrently
1. likewise	1. cycle
2. identical	2. cyclical
3. philosophy	3. dimensional
4. entity	4. identically
5. categorize	5. minimum
6. plus	6. principal
7. dimension	7. stabilize
8. stable	8. unified
9. category	9. unify

Collocations Chart

Verb	Adjective	Noun	Adverb
escape, break, complete	life, billing, monthly, weekly, economic, business	cycle	.........,,,, ,,,,.........
	cyclical	pattern, trend	
run, do, operate	....	....	concurrently
....	minimum	number, requirements, age, standards, sentence, wage, balance	....
....	principal	areas, concerns, means, source, reasons	....
remain	stable	economy, condition, prices, rates, currency, relationship	....
....	unified	country, system, theory, approach, community	....

D. The chart above shows some common collocations, or word partners, for selected target vocabulary. Refer to the chart and complete these sentences. Compare work with a partner.

1. The committee outlined the .... areas of concern to be discussed at the annual meeting.

2. Despite the unusually cold weather, fuel prices remained .... in January.

3. A student must meet the .... requirements to be admitted to the program.

4. The conference discussed the need to find a .... approach to combating email spam.

5. An economic or business .... is the regular fluctuations in economic activity over a period of time.

6. The study reported in *New Scientist* collected data suggesting that hurricane activity follows a .... pattern that lasts several decades.

7. By switching quickly between tasks, computers can have two or more programs running ....

8. You must maintain a .... balance of $500 in your account to avoid a service charge.

WRITING AND DISCUSSION TOPICS

1. Schoolbooks used to say that there are only four primary flavors—sweet, sour, bitter, and salt. There is growing evidence, however, that there may be others. Plus, there are other sensations in the mouth that contribute to taste. Design your own method of classifying taste. Think about what you know of the foods popular in different cultures. Explain your categorization system to your classmates in an essay or oral report. Consider displaying your system in a table or chart.

2. Human vision is keen enough to allow us to read, drive cars safely, aim and throw accurately, but it does have limitations. We often misjudge size, distance, shape, and intensity of light. Study these optical illusions. Why do these images fool our eyes? Present your ideas to the class.

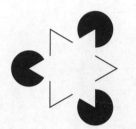

a. How many triangles?

c. The background is a gradient. Is the bar a gradient too?

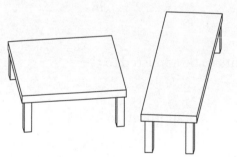

b. Which table is longer? Which one is wider? Did you measure them?

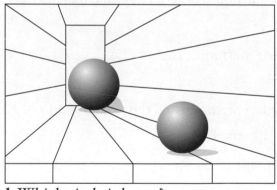

d. Which circle is larger?

BOOM AND BUST

In this unit, you will

➲ read about economic bubbles, including a rather unusual one that occurred hundreds of years ago.

➲ learn language for describing trends.

➲ learn language for summarizing.

➲ increase your understanding of the target academic words for this unit:

accurate	compound	estate	infrastructure	specify
attitude	denote	file	norm	trend
commodity	dispose	ideology	secure	underlie

SELF-ASSESSMENT OF TARGET WORDS

Think carefully about how well you know each target word in this unit. Then, write it in the appropriate column in the chart. When you've finished this unit, come back and reassess your knowledge of the target words.

I have never seen the word before.	I have seen the word but am not sure what it means.	I understand the word when I see or hear it in a sentence.	I have tried to use the word, but I am not sure I am using it correctly.	I use the word with confidence in either speaking *or* writing.	I use the word with confidence, both in speaking *and* writing.

BEFORE YOU READ

Read these questions. Discuss your answers in small groups.

1. People sometimes buy collectible items such as paintings or comic books because they hope to "make a killing"—or earn a lot of money—by reselling them when the price goes up. Can you think of any collectible items where that has been the case? Can you think of any cases where collectors "lost their shirts"—or lost all the money they invested?

2. Are there any investments that are "sure things"—ones that are safe and usually make money?

3. Here are several popular sayings that could relate to buying and selling. Discuss the possible meanings of these sayings. Are they good advice?

   Don't count your chickens before they hatch.

   A fool and his money are soon parted.

   Don't look a gift horse in the mouth.

   The early bird gets the worm.

   Nothing ventured, nothing gained.

   Don't throw good money after bad.

MORE WORDS YOU'LL NEED

asset: something with monetary value that a person or organization controls such as buildings, machinery, stocks, cash, or inventory

momentum: an object has momentum if its current speed will carry it farther even if no more force is applied. Prices and popular ideas are also said to have momentum.

speculator: someone who buys and sells things at increased risk in hopes of making a greater profit

READ

This article explains the phenomenon of economic bubbles and what causes them to burst.

Economic Bubbles

An economic bubble occurs when speculation in **commodities** (such as oil), **securities** (such as stocks and bonds), real **estate,** or collectibles drives up prices well beyond the item's intrinsic
5 value. The end result of this *boom* in price is a *crash* or *bust*. The price falls sharply once it becomes clear that it is far beyond the purchasing power of potential customers.

Speculators risk money in such investments
10 because they hope that price of an asset they purchased will quickly increase. Since most speculators are nervous about where they invest their money, bubbles are by no means the **norm**. After all, speculators face the danger that

15 the item is already overpriced. They also know that rising prices will encourage either greater production of a commodity or greater willingness of current owners to sell. Either of these conditions can serve as a "negative feedback"

20 mechanism that adjusts prices downward. In economic situations, negative feedback works a bit like your eyes do. As the light gets brighter, your pupils get smaller and let in less light. But what if your eyes worked as a "positive feedback"

25 mechanism? In sunlight, your pupils would open wide and damage the retina.

Economic bubbles occur when prices **trending** sharply upward serve as a positive, rather than a negative, feedback mechanism. For whatever

30 reason (fear of shortages, greed, an excessively optimistic **attitude** toward the future, or misinformation about an asset's **underlying** value), buyers believe that the value of the asset will continue to rise well beyond the current

35 price. If the price rises, exuberant speculators buy more, or those who missed out on the lower price want to buy before the price rises any higher. Some economists offer the "greater fool theory" to explain this: Buyers justify the high price they

40 pay by assuring themselves that they will find "a greater fool" who will pay even more. Or buyers assume that a rising trend has a momentum that will surely carry it higher. Under the right conditions, prices can reach dizzying heights

45 before falling. One famous example of this phenomenon is the tulip-buying bubble centered in Amsterdam in the 1630s when a single tulip bulb could cost a year's salary (see Reading 2).

Most bubbles cause little or no economic

50 damage. The losers (the "greater fools") are a bit wiser, and the winners (the sellers) are a lot richer. But the effects of a bubble might be felt more widely if the holders of the overpriced asset feel rich and spend foolishly. Imagine this:

55 You buy a house for $200,000 for which you borrowed $160,000. At this point, you have $40,000 in equity in the house (the difference between the price of the house and what you owe). The market value rises to $500,000 over

60 a 5-year period. Now you have $340,000 in equity ($500,000 – $160,000), so you borrow another $240,000 from a bank using this equity to secure the loan. You suddenly feel much wealthier. You control assets worth half a million

65 dollars. You still have $100,000 in equity in your home, and you have $240,000 to spend. And you do—a down payment on a vacation home, your daughter's freshman year at an expensive private college, a new car, and luxurious home

70 furnishings.

The market holds long enough for you to spend the money. Then it crashes and the value of your home falls to $325,000. Now you have negative equity and owe the bank almost $400,000. You

75 ask yourself why you should be paying $400,000 for a $325,000 house, so you stop paying your loan and give your house, car, and vacation home to the bank. Depending on how this plays out, the bank or you or both will take a huge loss. If

80 this situation is widespread, banks can fail and less money is available for the investments and purchases necessary to "grow" the economy.

Besides real estate bubbles, there are stock market bubbles. In a normal market, investors

85 buy stock in a company (also called "buying shares") because they anticipate that future profits will be distributed to shareholders, or because they believe that the value of the company's assets will increase. The share price

90 depends on how certain investors are that these gains will materialize—and uncertainty usually is enough to keep prices within reason. Sometimes, though, a "herd mentality[1]" sets in and too many investors rush to buy, driving prices to levels

95 that prove unrealistic. Eventually, the price collapses. When this happens to many companies simultaneously, it is called a stock market crash, with panicked investors selling so much stock that the market can drop a staggering amount in a

100 single day.

---

[1] *herd mentality*: idiom; compares people to a herd (group) of animals that thoughtlessly follows a leader

A recent stock market bubble was the "dot-com" bubble in the United States which lasted from the mid 1990s to 2001. Excitement about the economic possibilities of the Internet
105 encouraged investors to fund the creation of many dot-com companies—too many it turns out. For several years, instant wealth seemed within reach of any business with a website. Dot-com companies used expensive TV commercials
110 to attract investors, sometimes without indicating what product they were selling. Many companies, to increase "market share,"[2] purposely sold products at a loss, a scheme they believed would increase the company's customer
115 base and lead to future profits. Instead on March 10, 2000, the dot-com boom reached its peak when the NASDAQ Composite Index[3] (a number that reflects the value of stocks traded on the technology-heavy NASDAQ stock

120 exchange[4]) hit 5,132.52. Over the next two and a half years, the index dropped to as low as 1,108. Most of the dot-coms were out of business, **filing** for bankruptcy[5] or selling off their assets to healthier companies. Particularly hard-hit were
125 communication companies that invested heavily in a high-speed communications **infrastructure** that greatly exceeded demand.

Bubbles are not limited to real estate or glamorous "get rich" stock offerings. In 1996,
130 a series of stuffed animal toys called Ty Beanie Babies™ became such a fad that speculators bought up large quantities, assuming that their value as collectibles would rise greatly in future years. Did anyone make money on that fad?
135 Maybe, but why not see for yourself? Check out the price of Beanie Babies in an online auction site and decide if any of these sellers have struck it rich.

---

[2] *market share*: the percentage of a market that one company controls
[3] The NASDAQ Composite Index shows the relative stock market value of over 3000 companies listed on the NASDAQ stock exchange. This exchange includes many technology companies.
[4] *stock exchange*: a place where stocks and bonds are bought and sold
[5] *bankruptcy*: the legal condition of being unable to pay off debts; financial ruin

READING COMPREHENSION

Mark each sentence as *T* (true) or *F* (false) according to the information in Reading 1. Use the dictionary to help you understand new words.

.... **1.** The reading implies that economic bubbles can seriously alter one's attitude about spending money.

.... **2.** According to the reading, economic bubbles are the norm in a market-based economy.

.... **3.** The reading implies that in the end no one makes money as the result of an economic "bubble."

.... **4.** The reading says that the dot-com bubble led to widespread economic disaster.

.... **5.** We can infer from the reading that under normal conditions speculators tend to invest cautiously.

.... **6.** The reading suggests that selling items below cost in order to gain market share is a poor business model.

READING STRATEGY: Describing Trends

A *trend* is an increase or decrease in a behavior over a period of time. Here is a list of verbs useful for describing trends:

climb	drop	increase	reach
decline	fall	pass	rise
decrease	grow	peak at	top

This paragraph provides a more detailed description of the NASDAQ stock market bubble described in Reading 1. First, scan the paragraph to get a sense of the direction of the trends. Then, complete each sentence with an appropriate verb in the correct form. The same verb may be used more than once.

The NASDAQ Composite Index (1) .... and fell sharply between 1995 and 2003. On July 17, 1995, the index (2) .... 1,000 for the first time. Over the next four years, the market (3) .... steadily, (4) .... to over 2200 by January 1999. Over the next 15 months, it (5) .... even more rapidly, more than doubling its value. Finally, on March 10, 2000, it (6) .... 5,132. And then the bubble burst. Over the next two and a half years, the NASDAQ (7) .... dramatically to less than one-fourth of its peak value. On October 10, 2002, it (8) .... its lowest point since passing the 1,000 mark, (9) .... to 1,108.

VOCABULARY ACTIVITIES

Noun	Verb	Adjective	Adverb
attitude	....	attitudinal	attitudinally
commodity 상품	....	....	....
부지 estate 사유지	....	....	....
file	file	....	....
사회기반 infrastructure	....	....	....
norm 표준	....	....	....
security insecurity	secure	secure insecure	securely
trend	trend	trendy	....

A. Read these comments on investing. Fill in the blanks with a target word from the chart on page 85 that completes the sentence in a grammatical and meaningful way. Be sure to use the correct form.

1. Organizations can borrow money by issuing bonds, a kind of ....*security*....... .
   A bond is a borrower's promise to repay the principal with interest at a future
   date.

2. Cities or states often issue *municipal bonds* to raise money for ....*infrastructure*....
   improvements, such as new highways, schools, or other public projects.

3. The amount of interest a bond pays depends mainly on the risk the investor faces.
   The higher the risk, the higher the interest rate. Municipal bonds are relatively
   ....*secure*.............; thus they tend to pay a lower interest rate.

4. Investors have different ....*commodity*........... toward risk. To help investors assess
   risk, bonds are rated from AAA, the most secure, to D, the least secure.

5. Investing in bonds issued by a corporation is somewhat safer than buying stock
   in the corporation. If the corporation must ....*file*.......... for bankruptcy,
   bond holders are paid first, before the stockholders.

6. Today, one of the ....*trend*.......... investments is a "hedge fund." These rather
   mysterious funds make risky investments for small groups of wealthy investors.

7. Hedge funds invest very widely in stocks, bonds, currencies, real
   ....*estate*.......... , and ....*commodity*.......... such as wheat or oil.

B. Circle the word that best captures the meaning of the bold target word in each sentence.

1. The state board of education established new **norms** for children studying the
   language arts.
       a. usual behavior   **b.** standards to meet

2. The bookshelf was **secured** firmly to the wall.
       a. fastened   **b.** made safe

3. They **filed** the legal papers necessary for starting a corporation.
       a. stored documents   **b.** registered to begin a process

4. The legal battle over who would inherit her **estate** went on for many years.
       a. house and land   b. money and property

5. The fact that a large earthquake had not been felt since 1994 gave residents a false sense of **security**.

   a. freedom from risk   **b.** protective measures

6. The state passed a bond to build more prisons and improve the **security** at existing ones.

   a. a stock certificate   **b.** protective measures

7. Qualified math teachers are becoming a precious **commodity**.

   a. something useful   **b.** raw material that can be bought or sold

8. The magazine is devoted to covering **trends** in women's apparel.

   a. styles of fashion   **b.** general increases or decreases

C. In small groups, pick one area of contemporary life from the box and describe a trend that you see developing in it.

clothing fashions	television shows	careers
comic books	electronic media	recreation
popular music	the Internet	collectibles

READING 2

BEFORE YOU READ

Read these questions. Discuss your answers in small groups.

1. Mass hysteria is a situation in which a large number of people panic, act crazily, or show excessive excitement. Can you think of a situation where people displayed mass hysteria when a new product came out?

2. It is said that people will often do things in a crowd that they would never consider doing alone. Have you seen any evidence that this is true?

MORE WORDS YOU'LL NEED

botanist: a scientist who studies plant life

commerce: the buying and selling of goods on a large scale

propagate: to cause a plant or animal to multiply or breed

volatile: likely to change quickly and unpredictably. Financial investments or markets are sometimes volatile.

This article chronicles one of the most interesting economic bubbles in history.

Tulipomania

One of the most entertaining chapters in Charles Mackay's classic *Extraordinary Popular Delusions and the Madness of Crowds* (1841) concerns a speculative bubble that occurred in the Netherlands in the 1630s. What makes this bubble such a curiosity is that it concerned, of all things, tulips, a variety of flower grown from bulbs and noted for its vivid colors and striking patterns.

According to Mackay's account, in the mid-to-late 1500s tulips from Turkey made their way to Amsterdam, where they grew in popularity among wealthy people who would pay extravagant prices for the rarer varieties. The desire to possess them spread to the middle classes, and apparently people would spend a fortune to acquire a single root. The business in tulip bulbs was so great that by 1623 a single bulb could easily cost as much as a year's salary. And the rarest bulbs by 1635 could fetch as much as 40 times that. If Mackay's figures are correct, a single bulb of the prized *Admiral Liefken* variety was worth as much as 19 tons of butter or 440 "fat sheep." Apparently, owning such a prize **denoted** wealth and prestige.

Mackay enlivens his account with amusing anecdotes. A sailor, while delivering merchandise, idly stole a bulb of the prized *Semper Augustus* variety from a merchant, and thinking it was an onion, ate it along with a fish that the merchant had given him. The sailor was quietly sitting on a coil of ropes finishing the "onion" when the merchant finally caught up with him. In another episode, a visiting amateur botanist saw an interesting-looking root lying in a wealthy Dutchman's home. Unable to suppress his curiosity, he cut up the pricey *Admiral Van der Eyck* tulip to study it. The confused botanist, after being dragged by the collar to the local courthouse, found himself in prison until he could raise money to cover the owner's loss.

To accommodate the lively market for tulips, by 1636 several exchanges were established where buyers and sellers could acquire futures contracts (a promise to buy or sell a **specified** amount at a preset price). By buying and trading such contracts, tulip traders sought to profit from the fluctuation in tulip prices and grow instantly rich. The availability of easy credit and loans also facilitated buying. Similar to the "day-traders" during the dot-com craze of the late 1990s, who quit their jobs, borrowed money, and used their personal computers to trade volatile Internet and technology stocks, people converted their houses and land into cash in order to invest in the flowers. In small towns, taverns served as the local tulip commodity exchange.

But it was not to last. According to Mackay, once ordinary people bought tulips to sell for profit and not for planting in rich people's gardens, the price was bound to drop as the foolishness of it all became apparent. In late 1636, prices peaked and fell sharply. Sellers panicked and sold at any price, buyers defaulted on their futures contracts, and the easy credit that buyers could count on to fund their purchases dried up. Those who got out early ended up quietly rich, but many who believed themselves instantly rich were ruined. Mackay says commerce "suffered a severe shock," and took many years to recover.

Mackay's famous account serves as a warning to all those who speculate in stocks, real estate, or commodities. As investment brochures routinely say, "Past performance is no guarantee of future returns." But did Mackay exaggerate?

85 Was this really an extraordinary delusion and an example of the irrationality of crowds? Or was he too anxious to find another instance of what he called "the great and awful book of human folly?" Did the 17th century speculation in tulips 90 really do long-term damage to the country's economic infrastructure?

Recent writers and researchers have raised doubts about the scope of this bubble and believe a more **accurate** history of the period 95 better clarifies the reasons it occurred. In his book *Tulipomania* (1999), Mike Dash agrees the Dutch tulip market was a speculative bubble driven by inexperienced investors. But he also reveals why rational people might have become 100 caught up in it. The flowers had unique color patterns much in demand for their beauty, but each new variety had to be propagated from a single bulb which could only produce two bulbs in the next year, four after that, and so 105 on. When the available quantity was small, naturally the underlying value of a single bulb increased. The more abundant varieties sold cheaply by the pound. To complicate matters, the gorgeous markings on the most striking 110 bulbs were actually the result of a virus. That made them sickly and difficult to propagate. This biologically-determined rarity added to their value and kept prices higher than would normally be expected. Until 1634 or so, tulip 115 prices behaved normally, with rare, slowly propagating varieties more expensive than the plentiful varieties.

But how do we explain the 20-fold increase in price before the 1636–37 crash? Isn't such 120 an increase a sure sign of speculative madness? Researchers point out that Mackay's account leaves out mention of two events that may account for some of this fluctuation. In 1636–37, the bubonic plague[1] struck the Netherlands, 125 an event that must have had some effect on the collapsing prices of a luxurious commodity.

Mackay also neglects to mention the Thirty Years War in Europe. According to Thompson and Treussard of the University of California 130 at Los Angeles, this devastating conflict played havoc with tulip demand. In the early 1630s, after stabilizing victories, tulip sales rose in Germany, where they grew well, but the tides of war changed in 1636. Sales in Germany dropped, 135 and gardens were literally dug up to sell the bulbs to raise cash.

Thompson and Treussard place much of the blame on government policies. As the market fell due to plague and war, the government 140 allowed speculators to convert their futures contracts from an "obligation" to buy into an "option" to buy. In effect, sellers could not force buyers to honor their contracts. Without futures contracts to protect themselves against 145 price drops, holding tulips became riskier and the price dropped accordingly. Thompson and Treussard caution against the "popular delusion" conclusion of Mackay and say "tulipomania" was actually an example of how market forces 150 efficiently react to sudden changes in the prospects for profit and loss. Dash's book also makes it evident that, like the relatively mild recession[2] following the burst of the dot-com bubble, tulipomania's economic impact was 155 minor since only a fraction of the economy was devoted to tulip trading, with the Amsterdam exchange and others wanting no part of it.

Not all observers are willing to **dispose** of Mackay so readily. Kim Phillips-Fein, an 160 **ideologically** motivated critic of market-based economies writing at the height of the dot-com bubble, complains that "trendy academics like to say that the tulip craze wasn't a bubble at all." Favoring market-driven economies, these 165 researchers too easily dismiss the dangers of what she feared was a forthcoming economic disaster in western economies. Meanwhile, "contrarian"[3] investors will most likely continue

---

[1] *plague*: an epidemic disease transmitted by flea bites and usually spread by rats
[2] *recession*: a period of time when the economic activity of a region is declining
[3] *contrarian*: tending to take an opposing attitude or position

to use the tulip history to warn investors against a "herd mentality" that encourages people to buy overpriced stocks. And professional investors and financial analysts will point to tulipomania as a warning of what happens when amateurs make their own investment decisions.

Without a clear, agreed-upon chronology of events that led to the stunning rise and fall of tulip prices, we may never know the causes with any certainty, and any explanation may reveal more about the researcher's ideological bias than it does about Dutch life in 1636. Was tulipomania an example of mass hysteria and human foolishness? Was it an early indictment of market-driven economies? Is it a textbook example of how markets correct themselves, and a warning to governments not to interfere lest they **compound** the problem? Or is it simply a blip in history—where greed, fear, opportunity, a love for beautiful things, and bad luck converged to produce an improbable outcome?

Are there modern parallels? Tulips seem reasonably priced today, but what about star athletes? In the 1990s, the Chicago Bulls professional basketball team paid Michael Jordan tens of millions of dollars each year to play. Risky? Yes. But Jordan brought them six championships. In the 2005–2006 season, 46 players in the National Basketball Association earned $10,000,000 or more per season. Only one, Shaquille O'Neal of the Miami Heat, played for a championship team. "Hoopimania," perhaps?

READING COMPREHENSION

Mark each sentence as *T*(true) or *F*(false) according to the information in Reading 2. Use the dictionary to help you understand new words.

.... 1. Tulips are native to the Netherlands.

.... 2. Buying tulips was one way to show off one's wealth.

.... 3. The reading implies that tulip trading proved profitable for many people.

.... 4. Tulip trading was so hysterical that we must conclude that it seriously damaged the infrastructure of Amsterdam.

.... 5. The reading suggests that ideology plays a part in the conclusions that scholars draw about tulipomania.

READING STRATEGY: Summarizing

A. The first six paragraphs of Reading 1 offer a lengthy summary of a chapter in Charles Mackay's book *Extraordinary Popular Delusions and the Madness of Crowds*. The article also has shorter summaries of the work of other writers. Scan the article to find them.

1. Line numbers: ....

   Whose work is being summarized? ....

   What are the main points of the summary? ....

   ....

2. Line numbers: ....

   Whose work is being summarized? ....

   What are the main points of the summary? ....

A summary reports the ideas of another writer and should clearly indicate this source. The phrase "according to ..." is frequently used, but writers also employ a large inventory of reporting verbs with many shades of meaning. These verbs fall into two general categories.

Verbs Indicating Neutrality

This writer does not indicate agreement or disagreement with Mackay.

> *Charles Mackay **says** commerce "suffered a severe shock. . . ."*

argues	claims	reports	suspects
asserts	complains	says (that) ...	thinks
assumes	explains	states	
believes	maintains	suggests	

Verbs Indicating Agreement

This writer agrees that the researchers are stating a fact.

> *Researchers **point out** that Mackay's account leaves out mention of two events. . . .*

acknowledges	establishes	notices	reveals
admits	indicates	points out (that)...	shows
discloses	is aware that	proves	
discovers	knows	realizes	

B. Many readings in this book report another author's ideas. Write *N* if the reading remains neutral toward the reported (underlined) idea. Write *A* if the reading shows agreement. (Note: item 6 uses an expression not included in the box above.)

.... 1. Kim Phillips-Fein complains that "<u>trendy academics like to say that the tulip craze wasn't a bubble at all.</u>"

.... 2. In fact, Bramble and Lieberman maintain that <u>decades of research indicates that humans are very good runners indeed.</u>

.... 3. Hunt points out that <u>by the time detailed observations were made in the 19th century, the culture was virtually dead.</u>

.... 4. Hunt and Lipo suggest <u>the paths were built at different times by different groups of people.</u>

.... 5. Hunt and Lipo suspect that <u>stories of cannibalism could have been fabricated by the missionaries who arrived in 1864.</u>

.... 6. Dash's book also makes it evident that, <u>like the relatively mild recession following the burst of the dot-com bubble, tulipomania's economic impact was minor.</u>

VOCABULARY ACTIVITIES

Noun	Verb	Adjective	Adverb
accuracy	....	accurate inaccurate	accurately
compound	compound	compound	....
denotation	denote	....	....
disposal disposition	dispose of	disposed (to doing sth)	....
ideology	....	ideological	ideologically
specifics specification	specify	specific specified	specifically
....	underlie	underlying	....

A. Fill in the blanks with a target word from the chart that completes the sentence in a grammatical and meaningful way. Be sure to use the correct form.

1. A futures contract is a promise to buy or sell a certain asset or commodity at a fixed date in the future, at a .... price.

2. People buy or sell futures contracts to protect themselves from changes in the market price. Producers want protection because, if the price drops, they might be forced to .... of great quantities of the commodity at too low a price.

3. Likewise, consumers who will need large quantities of the commodity at a later date want protection if the .... value of that commodity rises greatly.

4. Speculators think that they can profit from trading futures contracts if they can .... predict the price of a commodity at a future date.

5. It is easy for critics who are .... opposed to this type of investing to find fault with the short-term thinking of speculators. They argue that a government agency should determine a fair price.

6. Defenders of free markets argue that governments, if they interfere too much with pricing, may actually .... the problems that producers and consumers face.

B. Which meaning of the word *compound* is expressed in each sentence? Match the sentence on the left with the definition on the right. Compare answers with a partner.

.... 1. The lesson today covered how to punctuate compound sentences.

a. to engage in actions that make sth worse

.... 2. After getting her fourth traffic ticket, she compounded her legal problems by forgetting to pay the fine.

b. to pay interest on both money invested and the accumulated interest

.... 3. To calculate how many years of compounding it will take for your investment to double in value, divide the interest rate into 72. With six percent interest, it will take 12 years.

c. containing two or more parts or elements (usually technical)

.... 4. Many plants, such as bean plants, have compound leaves.

d. two or more things joined or combined

In analyzing words that have rich psychological and emotional meanings, teachers often make a distinction between *denotation* (the dictionary meaning of the word) and *connotation* (what the word symbolizes or "evokes").

In common usage, expect to hear people use the words *denote, symbolize, stand for, signify,* or *represent* to indicate symbolic meanings or connotations. For example,

*In many cultures, displaying the palm of the right hand **denotes** friendship or lack of aggression.*

C. In a small group, discuss possible symbolic meanings that each word or phrase could have in a poem or song. In your answers, practice using the words *denote, symbolize, stand for, signify,* or *represent*.

1. a rose

   A rose is a kind of flower that symbolizes passion and love.

2. autumn leaves   5. a bright yellow tulip

3. a raven   6. a single wolf hunting in winter

4. a deep, cold lake   7. a distant mountain

Collocations Chart

Verb	Adjective	Noun	Prepositional Phrase
....	positive, negative, healthy, bad	*attitude*	to / toward sth
compound	....	problem, difficulty, error, effect, interest, dividends	....
dispose of	....	waste, objections	....
file	....	complaint, report, claim, lawsuit, tax return, application, documents, papers	....
conform to, deviate from, depart from	established, accepted, cultural, social, ethical	(the) *norm*(s)	of society, behavior, family life
....	*specific*	example, information, issue, question, problem, reason, course of action, area, time	....
....	*underlying*	message, theme, problem, cause, difference, factor, patterns, assumption, trend	....

D. The chart above shows some common collocations, or word partners, for selected target vocabulary. Refer to the chart and complete these sentences.

1. The professor asked us to analyze the .... themes in the story.

2. The teacher instilled a positive .... toward literature in her students.

3. They .... a complaint with the Commodities Futures Trading Commission for misconduct.

4. All of the objections to the plan were .... quickly.

5. The operations committee outlined a .... course of action to address the falling stock price.

6. Efforts to control the flow of traffic through the city only served to .... the problem.

7. All members are expected to conform to established .... of ethical behavior.

WRITING AND DISCUSSION TOPICS

A. Write a group story:

Each student in a small group is assigned one set of words from the box. On a loose piece of paper, write the first line of a story featuring a word from your set of words.

Pass your paper to the left and receive a paper from the right.

Using another word from your set, continue the story you just received.

Continue this process until you have added to every story. Read the stories aloud.

1	2	3	4
confer	fundamental	manipulate	prime
transmit	category	dimension	likewise
entity	minimum	plus	unify
accurate	compound	estate	infrastructure
norm	trend	commodity	dispose
intrinsically	project	refinement	theory
cyclical	stabilize	accuracy	security
5	**6**	**7**	**8**
diminish	incorporate	physical	refine
likewise	philosophy	stable	concurrent(ly)
cycle	identical	parameter	principal
specify	attitude	denote	file
ideology	secure	underlie	foundation
theorize	stressful	categorize	dimensional
trendy	inaccurate	conference	stability

B. Discuss or write in response to these items.

1. Write a one-paragraph summary of the second half of the article "Tulipomania." Begin with this sentence:

   According to the article, more recent writers and researchers have raised questions about Mackay's account. Mike Dash…

2. Research one of these economic organizations or types of investments and explain what it is or does.

The New York Stock Exchange	a bond
The Securities and Exchange Commission	a common stock
The World Bank	a mutual fund
Foreign Exchange Market	an option contract
a money market fund	an IPO (initial public offering)

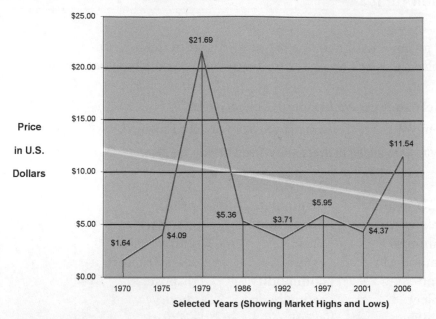

Annual Average Price of Silver, 1970-2006

Price in U.S. Dollars

$25.00

$20.00 — $21.69

$15.00

$11.54

$10.00

$5.95

$5.36

$5.00 — $4.09 — $3.71 — $4.37

$1.64

$0.00

1970 1975 1979 1986 1992 1997 2001 2006

Selected Years (Showing Market Highs and Lows)

3. Look at the graph above and analyze the trends it describes. Write a paragraph describing the dramatic increase and decrease in silver prices that occurred in the late 1970s and early 1980s.

4. The graph above shows that silver prices began rising again in 2001. Is another silver bubble forming? Do additional research on recent silver prices and write a paragraph explaining what you think.

5. In your opinion, are there currently any economic bubbles developing in the world? Think about things like real estate values, the stock market, and popular collectibles. Go online and do research. Give statistical evidence to support your opinion.

Unit 7 Sociology

DECISIONS, DECISIONS

In this unit, you will

- ➲ read about two different approaches to decision-making.
- ➲ evaluate generalizations.
- ➲ learn about uses of analogies.
- ➲ increase your understanding of the target academic words for this unit:

adapt	deduce	hypothesis	mode	respond
conform	enforce	implicate	nonetheless	statistic
consent	exclude	imply	option	thesis

SELF-ASSESSMENT OF TARGET WORDS

Think carefully about how well you know each target word in this unit. Then, write it in the appropriate column in the chart. When you've finished this unit, come back and reassess your knowledge of the target words.

I have never seen the word before.	I have seen the word but am not sure what it means.	I understand the word when I see or hear it in a sentence.	I have tried to use the word, but I am not sure I am using it correctly.	I use the word with confidence in either speaking *or* writing.	I use the word with confidence, both in speaking *and* writing.

BEFORE YOU READ

Read these questions. Discuss your answers in small groups.

1. When you are treated for an illness or injury, do you feel more comfortable if the medical doctor quickly determines what you are suffering from or if the doctor takes a long time?

2. Some decisions are made quickly. Some are more deliberate. Examine the items below and decide whether a quick decision or long deliberation is better.

- making a move in a game like chess
- choosing a movie to see
- deciding whether to trust a stranger
- deciding what clothing to buy
- choosing a college or university
- electing a leader of a club or organization
- deciding to accept a job
- deciding whether someone is guilty of a crime

MORE WORDS YOU'LL NEED

diagnosis: the act of identifying the cause of an illness or other problem

hunch: a feeling or guess that something is true not based on known facts

spontaneous: describing something done suddenly without much thought or planning

the unconscious: a part of the mind that we are not directly aware of

READ

In this excerpt from Malcolm Gladwell's *Blink: The Power of Thinking Without Thinking*, the author discusses research into the validity of hunches.

Blink

In front of you are four decks of cards—two of them red and the other two blue. Each card in those four decks either wins you a sum of money or costs you some money, and your job is to turn
5 over cards from any of the decks, one at a time, in such a way that maximizes your winnings. What you don't know at the beginning, however, is that the red decks are a minefield.[1] The rewards are high, but when you lose on
10 the red cards, you lose a lot. Actually, you can win by only taking cards from the blue decks, which offer a nice steady diet of $50 payouts and

modest penalties. The question is how long will it take you to figure this out?

15 Scientists at the University of Iowa did this experiment a few years ago. They found that after we've turned over about fifty cards, most of us start to develop a hunch about what's going on. After about eighty cards, most of
20 us have figured out the game and can explain exactly why the two red decks are such a bad idea. That much is straightforward. We have some experiences. We think them through. We develop a **hypothesis**. We **deduce** A from B.
25 That's the way learning works.

---

[1] *minefield*: literally, an area where explosive devices (mines) have been placed. Here, it refers to something full of potential dangers.

But the Iowa scientists did something else. They hooked each gambler up to a machine that measured the activity of the sweat glands below the skin in the palms of their hands. Like most of our sweat glands, those in our palms **respond** to stress as well as temperature. The Iowa scientists found that gamblers started generating stress responses to the red decks by the tenth card, forty cards before they were able to say that they had a hunch about what was wrong with those two decks. More importantly, right around the time their palms started sweating, their behavior began to change as well. They started favoring the blue cards and taking fewer and fewer cards from the red decks.

The Iowa experiment **implies** that our brain uses two very different strategies to make sense of the situation. The first is the one we're most familiar with. It's the conscious strategy. We think about what we've learned, and eventually we come up with an answer. But it takes us eighty cards to get there. It's slow, and it needs a lot of information. There's a second strategy, though. It operates a lot more quickly. It starts work after ten cards, and it's really smart, because it picks up the problem with the red decks almost immediately. It has the drawback[2], however, that it operates—at least at first— entirely below the surface of consciousness. It sends its messages through weirdly indirect channels, such as the sweat glands in the palms of our hands. It's a system in which our brain reaches conclusions without immediately telling us that it's reaching conclusions.

The part of our brain that leaps to conclusions like this is called the **adaptive** unconscious, and the study of this kind of decision-making is one of the most important new fields in psychology. The adaptive unconscious can be thought of as a kind of giant computer that quickly and quietly processes a lot of the data we need in order to keep functioning as human beings. When you walk out into the street and suddenly realize that a truck is bearing down on you, do you have time to think through all your **options**? Of course not. The only way that human beings could ever have survived as a species for as long as we have is that we've developed another kind of decision-making apparatus that's capable of making very quick judgments based on very little information.

The psychologist Timothy D. Wilson in his book *Strangers to Ourselves* says that we toggle back and forth between our conscious and unconscious **modes** of thinking, depending on the situation. A decision to invite a coworker over for dinner is conscious. You think it over. You decide it will be fun. You ask him or her. The spontaneous decision to argue with that same coworker is made unconsciously—by a different part of the brain and motivated by a different part of your personality.

Whenever we meet someone for the first time, whenever we interview someone for a job, whenever we react to a new idea, whenever we're faced with making a decision quickly, we use that second part of our brain. How long, for example, did it take you, when you were in college, to decide how good a teacher your professor was? A class? Two classes? A semester? The psychologist Nalini Ambady gave students three ten-second videotapes of a teacher—with the sound turned off—and found they had no difficulty at all coming up with a rating of the teacher's effectiveness. When Ambady cut the clips[3] back to five seconds, and even two seconds, the ratings were essentially the same. A person watching a silent two-second video clip of a teacher he or she has never met will reach conclusions similar to those of a student who has sat in the teacher's class for an entire semester. That's the power of our adaptive unconscious.

I think we are innately suspicious of this kind of rapid cognition. We assume that the quality of a decision is directly related to the time and effort that went into making it. When doctors

---

[2] *drawback*: disadvantage
[3] *clip*: short scene, usually on film

face a difficult diagnosis, they order more tests, and when we are uncertain about what we hear, we ask for a second opinion. And what do we 115 tell our children? Haste makes waste. Look before you leap. Stop and think. Don't judge a book by its cover. We believe that we are always better off gathering as much information as possible and spending as much time as possible 120 in deliberation. We really only trust conscious decision-making. But there are moments, particularly in times of stress, when haste does not make waste, when our snap judgments and first impressions can offer a much better means 125 of making sense of the world. Decisions made very quickly can be every bit as good as decisions made cautiously and deliberately.

READING COMPREHENSION

A. Mark each sentence as *T* (true) or *F* (false) according to the information in Reading 1. Use the dictionary to help you understand new words.

.... 1. In the experiment with the red and blue decks of cards, most people had some idea of what was happening after fifty cards.

.... 2. People became suspicious of the red deck of cards even before they could explain why.

.... 3. According to the reading, the unconscious brain works more slowly than the conscious brain.

.... 4. Most people make all of their decisions in either one mode or the other, not both.

.... 5. The decision to jump out of the way of a moving truck is probably an unconscious one.

.... 6. The sayings in the last paragraph of the article all urge people to think carefully before making a decision.

.... 7. The reading suggests that we underestimate the value of snap judgments.

.... 8. Our brains do not work well when information is limited.

B. Scan the reading to find the sentences paraphrased below. In the blank, write the first few words of the original sentence.

1. The majority of subjects began to suspect something after they'd played about fifty cards.

....

2. So far there were no surprises.

....

3. We reflect on what we know and in time we reach a conclusion.

....

4. But it has a disadvantage in that it initially takes place beyond the reaches of conscious thought.

....

5. It is like a huge microprocessor that silently and efficiently collects and analyzes a lot of necessary information.

....

READING STRATEGY: Evaluating Generalizations

Deduce, infer, conclude—these three verbs describe something our mind does constantly. We observe facts and figure out other things that must also be true. Some inferences we make are obviously true. No other conclusion is possible.

All adult birds have feathers. A gadwall is a kind of bird. So gadwalls no doubt have feathers.

Sometimes, though, our inference is based on evidence that is less *conclusive*.

Almost all species of bird can fly. Since a gadwall is a bird, it can probably fly.

We add "probably" because of the slight statistical chance that a gadwall (a duck-like bird) is a flightless bird.

Likewise, a generalization may describe something that is true in all cases or it may indicate a statistical tendency.

Malcolm Gladwell uses these generalizations to support his conclusion that we should place more trust in first impressions. Write *T* for those statements that describe something that is true for all people and *S* for those that illustrate a statistical tendency. Write *N* if you're not sure.

.... 1. After we've turned over about fifty cards, most of us start to develop a hunch about what's going on. After about eighty cards, most of us have figured out the game.

.... 2. The adaptive unconscious ... quietly processes a lot of the data we need in order to keep functioning as human beings.

.... 3. ... we toggle back and forth between our conscious and unconscious modes of thinking, depending on the situation.

.... 4. A person watching a silent two-second video clip of a teacher he or she has never met will reach conclusions similar to those of a student who has sat in the teacher's class for an entire semester.

.... 5. We really only trust conscious decision-making.

VOCABULARY ACTIVITIES

Noun	Verb	Adjective	Adverb
adaptation adaptability	adapt	adaptable adapted	....
deduction	deduce	deducible	....
hypothesis	hypothesize	hypothetical	hypothetically
implication	imply	implied	....
mode	....	....	....
option	opt	optional	optionally
response	respond	responsive	responsively

A. Read the paragraph about "thin-slicing." Fill in the blanks with a target word from the chart above that completes the sentence in a grammatical and meaningful way. Be sure to use the correct form.

"Thin-slicing" is the ability of our unconscious mind to (1) .... characteristics of a person's behavior and personality from a very brief encounter. It is called thin-slicing because just a "slice" of experience may be all that is necessary for us to form an accurate impression of someone and (2) .... quickly to a new situation. Thin-slicing is vital for operating successfully in a fast-changing environment. Because it is unconscious and automatic, we can size up a person quickly, instantly narrow our (3) .... for dealing with this person and decide on an appropriate (4) ....

Movies and television programs make good use of our ability to thin-slice. When new characters appear, our brain is in "thin-slice" (5) .... A brief glimpse or several lines of dialog can (6) .... much about a character's personality, background, and importance. We are suspicious of these first impressions, of course, because moviemakers try to trick us. But that is part of the fun.

A *hypothesis* is an unproven statement that makes a claim, usually about causes or effects. To test a hypothesis, first we ask what this hypothesis *implies*.

*If this **hypothesis** is true, what other things have to be true?*

If these other things have to be true for the hypothesis to be true, we say that they are *deducible*. For example, if someone claims a medicine cures baldness, we can *deduce* the following:

If bald-headed people take this medicine, their hair will grow back.

This prediction about hair growth is deducible. It has to be true if the medicine actually works. The next step is to test whether the prediction proves true. If the prediction proves false (hair does not grow back), then we know the hypothesis is also false. We can exclude this hypothesis from further consideration.

B. Using your powers of deductive reasoning, complete the sentence with a prediction that would have to be true if the hypothesis is true.

1. Hypothesis: Emotions originate in the heart.

   This claim implies that *people with artificial hearts will lack emotions.*

2. Hypothesis: Music is a basic part of being human.

   If this is true, we can predict that ....

3. Hypothesis: Drinking a small amount of coffee temporarily improves memory.

   From this statement, we can deduce that ....

4. Hypothesis: Humans are good at concentrating on two challenging tasks at the same time.

   If this hypothesis is true, then ....

C. Your prediction may be deducible, but can it be tested? Design an experiment or test for one of your predictions in activity B. Explain your test to the class.

D. In colleges and universities, students have required courses and electives, or optional courses. Examine this list of college courses. Write *R* for the courses you feel should be required for all students and *O* for those that should be optional.

.... astronomy   .... literature   .... psychology

.... biology   .... music appreciation .... sociology

.... business   .... philosophy   .... women's studies

.... a foreign language .... political science   .... world history

In a small group, discuss your ideas and come to a consensus on required and optional courses. Share your group's decision with the class.

BEFORE YOU READ

Here is a list of decisions similar to the ones you examined before you read *Blink*. This time, ask yourself if you would be more likely to trust a decision made by a single expert or a consensus reached by a larger group of people. Discuss your ideas in a small group.

- making a move in a game like chess
- choosing a movie to see
- choosing a restaurant to dine at
- deciding what clothing to buy
- choosing a college or university
- electing the leader of a club or organization
- choosing a leader to solve a temporary problem
- predicting what team will win a championship
- deciding whether someone is guilty of a crime

MORE WORDS YOU'LL NEED

impromptu: done without rehearsal or planning

understatement: something stated in a restrained way when the facts would allow for a stronger statement; the opposite of exaggeration

wager: money that is bet or gambled on the outcome of a contest, or future event

READ

This excerpt from *The Wisdom of Crowds*, by James Surowiecki, discusses the benefits of collective thinking.

The Wisdom of Crowds

One day in 1906, the British scientist Francis Galton headed for a country fair in the town of Plymouth where the local farmers and townspeople gathered to appraise the quality
5 of each other's cattle, sheep, chickens, horses, and pigs. Examining workhorses and prize hogs may seem a strange way for a scientist to spend an afternoon, but there was a certain logic to it. Galton was a man obsessed with two things: the
10 measurement of physical and mental qualities, and breeding. And livestock shows are all about good and bad breeding.

Breeding mattered to Galton because he believed that only a very few people had the
15 characteristics necessary to keep societies

healthy. He had devoted much of his career to measuring those characteristics and **developing** statistical procedures and formulas for doing so. His experiments left him with little faith in the
20 intelligence of the average person, "the stupidity and wrong-headedness of many men and women being so great as to be scarcely credible." Only if power and control stayed in the hands of the select, well-bred few, Galton believed, could a
25 society remain healthy and strong.

As he walked through the exhibition that day Galton came across a weight-judging competition. A fat ox had been placed on display, and members of a gathering crowd were lining
30 up to place wagers on what the weight of the ox would be after it had been "slaughtered and

dressed." For sixpence, you could buy a stamped and numbered ticket, where you filled in your name, your address, and your estimate. The best guesses would receive prizes.

Eight hundred people tried their luck. "Many non-experts competed," Galton wrote later in the scientific journal *Nature*, "like those clerks and others who have no expert knowledge of horses, but who bet on races, guided by newspapers, friends, and their own fancies[1]." The analogy to a democracy, in which people of radically different abilities and interests each get one vote, had suggested itself to Galton immediately. "The average competitor was probably as well fitted for making a just estimate of the dressed weight of the ox, as an average voter is of judging the merits of most political issues on which he votes," he wrote.

To test this hypothesis, Galton turned the competition into an impromptu experiment. When the contest was over, the organizers **consented** to give Galton all the tickets, and he ran a series of statistical tests on them. After **excluding** 13 tickets with illegible answers, Galton then added all the contestants' estimates and calculated the mean[2] of the group's guesses. That number represented, you could say, the collective wisdom of the Plymouth crowd. If the crowd were a single person, that was how much it would have guessed the ox weighed.

Galton undoubtedly thought that the average guess of the group would be way off the mark. But Galton was wrong. The crowd guessed that the ox would weigh 1,197 pounds. After it had been slaughtered and dressed, it weighed 1,198 pounds. In other words, the crowd's judgment was essentially perfect. Perhaps breeding did not mean so much after all. Galton wrote later: "The result seems more creditable to the trustworthiness of a democratic judgment than

might have been expected." That was, to say the least, an understatement.

Francis Galton stumbled on a simple, but powerful, truth: under the right circumstances, groups are remarkably intelligent, and are often smarter than the smartest people in them. Even if most of the people within a group are not especially well-informed or rational, it can still reach a collectively wise decision. This is a good thing, since human beings are not perfectly designed decision makers. We generally have less information than we'd like. We have limited foresight into the future. Most of us lack the ability—and the desire—to make sophisticated cost-benefit calculations[3]. Instead of insisting on finding the best possible decision, we will often accept one that seems good enough. And we often let emotion affect our judgment. Yet despite all these limitations, when our imperfect judgments are aggregated in the right way, our collective intelligence is often excellent.

This intelligence, or what I'll call "the wisdom of crowds," is at work in the world in many different guises[4]. It's the reason the Internet search engine Google can scan a billion web pages and find the one page that has the exact piece of information you were looking for. It's the reason it's so hard to make money betting on football games. The wisdom of crowds has something to tell us about why the stock market works (and about why, every so often, it stops working). The idea of collective intelligence is essential to good science. And it has the potential to make a profound difference in the way companies do business.

Charles Mackay would have scoffed at the idea that a crowd of people could know anything at all. Mackay was the Scottish journalist who, in 1841, published *Extraordinary Popular Delusions and the Madness of Crowds*, an endlessly

---

[1] *fancy*: desire, whim
[2] *mean*: statistical average
[3] *cost-benefit calculation*: an analysis that compares the total cost of something (usually a large project) with the total benefit derived from it
[4] *guise*: form, manner of appearance

entertaining chronicle of mass manias and collective follies. Mackay's **thesis** was that crowds were never wise. They were never even reasonable. Collective judgments were doomed to be extreme. "Men, it has been well said, think in herds," he wrote. "It will be seen that they go mad in herds, while they only recover their senses slowly and one by one." **Nonetheless**, the wisdom of crowds has a far more important and beneficial impact on our everyday lives than we or Charles Mackay recognize, and its **implications** for the future are immense.

One of the striking things about the wisdom of crowds is that even though its effects are all around us, it's easy to miss, and, even when it's seen, it can be hard to accept. Most of us, whether as voters or investors or consumers or managers, believe that valuable knowledge is concentrated in a very few hands. We assume that the key to solving problems or making good decisions is finding that one right person who will have the answer. Even when we see a large crowd of people, many of them not especially well-informed, do something amazing like, say, predict the outcomes of horse races, we are more likely to attribute that success to a few smart people in the crowd than to the crowd itself. As sociologists Jack R. Soil and Richard Larrick put it, we feel the need to "chase the expert." Chasing the expert is a mistake, and a costly one at that. We should stop hunting and ask the crowd instead. Chances are, it knows.

Mackay was right about the extremes of collective behavior: there are times—think of a riot, or a stock market bubble—when collective decisions are utterly irrational. And in the present, many groups struggle to make even mediocre decisions, while others wreak havoc with their bad judgment. The fact is, groups work well under certain circumstances, and less well under others. Groups generally need to **enforce** rules to maintain order and coherence, and when they're missing or malfunctioning, the result is trouble. Groups benefit from members talking to and learning from each other, but too much communication, paradoxically[5], can actually make the group as a whole less intelligent. While big groups are often good for solving certain kinds of problems, big groups can also be unmanageable and inefficient. Conversely, small groups are easy to run, but they risk having too little diversity of thought and too much consensus.

Diversity and independence are important because the best collective decisions are the product of disagreement and contest, not consensus or compromise. An intelligent group does not ask its members to **conform** to its positions in order to let the group reach a decision everyone can be happy with. Instead, it figures out how to use mechanisms—like market prices, or intelligent voting systems—to produce collective judgments that represent not what any one person in the group thinks but rather, in some sense, what they all think. Paradoxically, the best way for a group to be smart is for each person in it to think and act as independently as possible.

---

[5] *paradoxically*: in a contradictory manner, often used to describe two pieces of evidence that seem to contradict each other

READING COMPREHENSION

Mark each sentence as *T* (true) or *F* (false) according to the information in Reading 2. Use the dictionary to help you understand new words.

.... 1. The reading suggests that Francis Galton contributed to the field of statistical measurement.

.... 2. Galton's original hypothesis about the intelligence of people was confirmed.

.... 3. James Surowiecki has reached a different conclusion about crowds from that of Charles Mackay.

.... 4. The best decisions are always made by people who are expert in a field.

.... 5. Surowiecki says groups are vulnerable to bad decision-making when there are rules that maintain order and focus.

.... 6. Surowiecki warns that group conformity can lead to poor judgments.

.... 7. This article tends to support the validity of democratic forms of government.

READING STRATEGY: Understanding Analogies

An *analogy* is a kind of comparison. It compares something we know little about to something that we know more about.

Writers use analogies for one of two reasons. They use analogies when something is difficult to grasp. In Unit 6, Reading 1 explains the effect of "negative" and "positive" feedback on the economy by comparing it to the more familiar subject of the eye:

> In economic situations, negative feedback works a bit like your eyes do. As the light gets brighter, your pupils get smaller and let in less light. But what if your eyes worked as a "positive feedback" mechanism? In sunlight, your pupils would open wide and damage the retina.

Writers also use analogies to make discoveries or to argue a point. The logic works like this:

- We don't know much about **A**.
- But we do know that **A** has similarities to **B**.
- Therefore, whatever is true of **B** may also be true of **A**.

James Surowiecki reports that Francis Galton used this kind of thinking in designing his weight-guessing experiment. Galton reasoned that if ordinary people could not guess something as simple as the weight of an ox, then they would, by analogy, make poor judgments on complex matters. But Galton's experiment showed the opposite. The group's average guess was amazingly accurate, so perhaps crowds make wise choices on complex matters as well.

Several readings in this book use analogies. Reread these selections and mark them with an *I* if the analogy is used to illustrate a difficult concept, or *A* if the analogy is used to argue a point.

.... 1. "Were Humans Born to Run?" (Unit 1) compares humans to other animals.

To understand how they can make this claim, let's consider what humans can do. The very best long distance runners can run five-minute miles for several hours. These efforts are amazing achievements, but even the casual jogger can often keep up an 8–10 minute a mile pace for several miles if not longer. Only a few animals of similar weight—large dogs, hyenas, wolves, and wildebeests— are capable of maintaining such speeds and actually prefer to trot a bit slower. Even a thousand-pound horse will not cover long distances any faster than a good recreational jogger.

.... 2. "Virtual Odors?" (Unit 5) compares odors to words.

In other words, smells function a bit like words do. We know thousands of different words, and the meaning of a word depends on the context in which it occurs. We define a word by pointing to the entity it refers to or by comparing its meaning to other words. With scents, we may say "it smells like a cucumber" or "it has a soapy smell."

.... 3. "Pitch and Timbre" (Unit 5) compares musical instruments to a mouth.

You can see the effect that an instrument's shape has on tone by considering what your mouth does when you make vowel sounds. If you sing the words "tea" and "too" and use the same musical note, the fundamental frequency is the same for both words. But "tea" sounds different because you changed the shape of your mouth in such a way as to dampen the overtones between about 500 Hz and 2,000 Hz. To make the vowel in the word "too," your mouth amplifies the overtones between 500 and 1,000 Hz and dampens the higher ones.

.... 4. "Tulipomania" (Unit 6) compares tulipomania to the dot-com bubble.

Dash's book also makes it evident that, like the relatively mild recession following the burst of the dot-com bubble, tulipomania's economic impact was minor since only a fraction of the economy was devoted to tulip trading, with the Amsterdam exchange and others wanting no part of it.

How effective do you think these analogies are? Can you think of any better ones?

VOCABULARY ACTIVITIES

Noun	Verb	Adjective	Adverb/Conjunction
conformity conformist	conform	....	....
consent consensus	consent	consenting consensual	consensually
enforcement	enforce	enforced	....
exclusion	exclude	excluded exclusive	exclusively
implication	implicate	implicated	....
....	....	....	nonetheless
statistic statistics statistician	....	statistical	statistically
thesis	....	....	....

A. Read this brief article on prediction markets. Fill in the blanks with a target word from the table that completes the sentence in a grammatical and meaningful way. Be sure to use the correct form.

In *The Wisdom of Crowds*, James Surowiecki praises a method for predicting the future called "predictions markets." Prediction markets allow individuals to buy contracts with either real money or play money to predict the outcome of events. Participants can wager, for example, on who will win a presidential election. If the "market" thinks that one candidate is likely to win, the bids for the contract are higher.

1. According to James Surowiecki, prediction markets clearly illustrate his

   .... that crowds can make better predictions than a "think tank"

   of experts can.

2. In prediction markets, no individual opinions are .... Everyone

   can give an opinion.

3. Also, since the group's decision is arrived at .... , no one is

   forced to change their opinion.

4. Since the group does not need to reach a .... , there is no

   pressure to .... to the thinking of a few dominant members of

   the group.

continued

5. Surowiecki feels that prediction markets have important .... for the way groups structure their decision-making.

6. Critics complain that there are ways to manipulate predictions markets. .... , economists find these markets highly interesting.

7. The Iowa Electronic Markets, sponsored by the University of Iowa, has predicted the results of presidential elections with more .... accuracy than traditional polling methods 75% of the time.

> The verb *implicate* can mean "involve someone in something criminal or scandalous" or "blame something as a cause." The noun form, *implication*, refers to the possible effect of a decision.
>
> *He was **implicated** in several financial scandals.*
>
> *Their research **implicates** an airborne virus as the cause of the flu.*
>
> *We need to consider the **implications** of our decision. Our decision has serious implications.*
>
> Earlier in this unit, we studied the verb *imply*. It means to state something indirectly. It has the same noun form, *implication*.
>
> *The candidate **implied** that her opponent was not telling the truth.*
>
> *The article's **implication** is that the mayor was slow to respond to the crisis.*

B. Rewrite these sentences using a form of *implicate* or *imply*. Compare work with a partner.

1. The mayor was involved in a scheme that misused public funds.
2. What might result from the city's plan to expand the airport?
3. He objected to a suggestion in the article that he caused the city's financial crisis.
4. Corrupt building inspectors were partially to blame for the building's collapse.
5. The report insinuates that the city council is not working hard enough.

C. A *thesis* is the technical term for the main idea that an essay or article is trying to explain or support. A *thesis statement* is a sentence that expresses the essay's main idea. How would you describe the thesis of the two readings in this unit? Complete these sentences in your notebook. Discuss your ideas with the class.

1. In *Blink*, Malcolm Gladwell claims that...
2. In *The Wisdom of Crowds*, James Surowiecki argues that...

Collocations Chart

Verb/Adverb	Adjective	Noun	Verb/Prepositional Phrase
adapt to	....	new rules, situations, change, changing times, changing needs, etc.	....
conform to	....	rules, expectations, pressure, standards, regulations, wishes	....
give, grant, have, obtain, refuse, require	....	*consent*	....
enforce	....	rules, standards, regulations	....
....	traditional, usual, dominant, main	*mode*	of travel, transport, transportation, communication, governance
have, examine, study, look at	available, best, no, the only, limited	*option*	....
give, make, receive, provoke, elicit	positive, negative, favorable, enthusiastic, correct, appropriate	*response*	to sth
collect, gather, supply, furnish, provide, analyze, examine	vital, reliable, accurate, surprising, precise, up-to-date, recent, updated, revealing, shocking	*statistics*	on sth

D. The chart above shows some common collocations, or word partners, for selected target vocabulary. Refer to the chart and complete these sentences. Compare work with a partner.

1. The dominant .... of transportation within the campus was bicycles.

2. The article furnished some rather surprising .... on the educational achievement of children in the program.

3. A child's participation in the program requires the .... of the parents.

4. The new regulations received a very negative .... from the state's businesses.

5. The business failed when it was unable to .... to changing markets.

continued

6. They examined the available .... and decided to sell the
company to one of their competitors.

7. Businesses had no choice but to .... to the new regulations or
stop doing business in the state.

8. As of yet, the state has no mechanism for .... these regulations.

E. Individually or in a small group, write grammatical and meaningful sentences that include these sequences of words.

1. ...usual...mode...travel

The usual mode of travel was by car or bus.

2. ...adapt to...the changing situation...

3. ...collect...statistics...on how many students...

4. ...elicit...a favorable response when...

5. ...obtain...the consent of...before...

6. ...only option...conform to...standards...

WRITING AND DISCUSSION TOPICS

1. Malcolm Gladwell claims that people do a great deal of thinking within the first two seconds of any encounter, and that this kind of thinking is reasonably accurate. What do you think? Should we trust our first impressions? Or should we train ourselves to delay making judgments? What about "love at first sight?"

2. James Surowiecki says that a crowd is most effective in making guesses and predictions when it does not know that it can be effective. How do you explain this apparent paradox?

3. James Surowiecki says that crowds produce bad judgments for several different reasons, including emotional factors. What emotional factors might affect the wisdom of a crowd?

4. Both Gladwell and Surowiecki use *anecdotal evidence* to support their theses. An anecdote is a brief story based on real life. In order to be convincing as evidence, an anecdote must seem typical, not unusual or exceptional. What anecdotes from your own life or experience could you use to support or challenge the claims of Gladwell or Surowiecki?

SEARCHING FOR SUCCESS

In this unit, you will

- ➲ read about the Internet search engine Google and its new way of doing business.
- ➲ learn about analyzing and developing criteria.
- ➲ increase your understanding of the target academic words for this unit:

bias	constant	format	investigate	relevant
clarify	distribute	formula	offset	scope
compute	edit	found	potential	

SELF-ASSESSMENT OF TARGET WORDS

Think carefully about how well you know each target word in this unit. Then, write it in the appropriate column in the chart. When you've finished this unit, come back and reassess your knowledge of the target words.

I have never seen the word before.	I have seen the word but am not sure what it means.	I understand the word when I see or hear it in a sentence.	I have tried to use the word, but I am not sure I am using it correctly.	I use the word with confidence in either speaking *or* writing.	I use the word with confidence, both in speaking *and* writing.

BEFORE YOU READ

Read these questions. Discuss your answers in small groups.

1. When you hear the name Google, do you have a positive, negative, or neutral attitude toward the company? Why?

2. Google's search engine is so successful that it collects billions of dollars of revenue each year. Yet its search engine is free. Where do you imagine Google's revenue comes from?

3. When you search the Internet, what factors do you consider when you select a search engine?

MORE WORDS YOU'LL NEED

query: a specific demand for information submitted to a web browser

rank: to put in order according to some predetermined system

READ

This article traces the history of one of the most successful new companies of our time.

Google: A Brief History

If you type into Google's search engine the question "How does Google work?," Google itself offers a curious explanation: PigeonRank. According to this obvious joke, Google uses clusters of trained pigeons to "**compute** the relative value of web pages faster than human **editors** or machine-based algorithms[1]." Pigeons, they tell us, can spot minute differences between web pages and will peck when a **relevant** result appears on the screen. Pages with more pecks move to the top of the list. Google assures us that the pigeons are well treated and not overworked.

Two things are clear. Google wants the workings of its successful page-ranking search engine to remain secret, and Google does not mind if you believe pigeons are involved. Fooling aside, what actually accounts for Google's success? How does the search engine, in 0.04 seconds, find 46,000,000 pages relating to "Batman" and put the ones you are most likely to be interested in near the top of the list? How does Google make any money doing this?

The Google story begins in 1996 at Stanford University in California. Two graduate students, Larry Page and Sergey Brin, wanted to find a better way to search websites. Current search engines ranked search results according to how frequently the search words appeared on a page. This approach had several disadvantages. Users had to sort through too many listings to find relevant information. Plus, people could trick search engines to get their page listed at the top of a search query. A user who types in "Batman" does not want to see an online

---

[1] *algorithm*: a complicated set of procedures for accomplishing a task. It is designed so that a specific initial condition will lead to a definite result.

Google founders Larry Page and Sergey Brin

gambling site at the top of the rankings. Larry Page and Sergey Brin hypothesized that a page is more valuable if other sites link to it. If someone links to a page, then the page has at least some
40 importance. If a very important website links to the page, that indicates even greater importance. So Brin and Page designed a search engine that could "crawl" the web, download every web page, and analyze its relevance using a secret,
45 **constantly** changing **formula**. Pages with higher scores get listed toward the top.

Unable to sell their search engine software at the $1 million asking price to companies like Yahoo!, the two left Stanford in the fall of 1998
50 to **found** Google.com. The obvious superiority of their search engine quickly attracted financial backing[2]. So the two set up a data center in a garage and several rooms of a house, a venue they soon outgrew as the popularity of their
55 search engine increased. In less than a year, prominent investors provided $25 million to aggressively grow the company and improve its search engine. Sergey Brin promised a perfect search engine that "will process and understand
60 all the information in the world" and without charging anyone to use it.

But could Google make money? A free search engine that worked well quickly attracted users, an increase of about 50 percent each month,
65 but that required investing in more computing

power, and expensive supercomputers could cost $800,000. To avoid this expense, Brin and Page purchased thousands of ordinary PCs. Using software they designed, they linked these
70 computers together to make the equivalent of dozens of supercomputers with impressive storage space—all this for about one-third the cost of what their competitors were paying for computing power. To deal with the inevitable
75 problem of individual computers failing, Brin and Page wrote software that simply ignored a failing computer rather than bothering to replace it. By locating computers in multiple locations and duplicating their functions, they
80 were protected against losing data when trouble occurred.

Even with operating costs kept down, the company still needed to generate cash. One obvious tactic was to sell advertising space
85 on Google's home page. By the end of 1999, Google averaged 7 million searches each day. But research showed that large banner ads[3] and pop-up ads seemed more annoying to the user than profitable for the advertiser. Users already
90 loved Google's uncluttered and easy-to-use home page. Why crowd it with ads for products that users were not interested in? Brin and Page had a second problem with ads. Advertisers did not want to spend on advertising unless their
95 ad was near the top of the search results. If Google pleased advertisers, relevance to the user would no longer be the primary page-ranking consideration.

Brin and Page's solution allows ads but does
100 not **bias** the page ranking results in favor of advertisers. The Google home page remains free of ads. On search results pages, ads are text-only and appear in a clearly marked "sponsored links" area along the right margin of the page. To place
105 an ad, advertisers bid on specific "keywords" that relate to the products they sell. If the user searches for "running shoes," a dozen or

---

[2] *backing*: support
[3] *banner ad*: a long, thin ad across all or part of a web page

more ads appear because advertisers suspect that the user wants to buy running shoes. If the user types in "gorilla species," few or no ads will appear since the user is most likely not interested in purchasing anything.

The cost of an ad ranges from a few cents per click to $30 or more, depending on how much advertisers are willing to bid. Since advertisers are charged only if the user clicks on their ads, advertisers must maintain an acceptable "click-through rate"[4] for each keyword. If the click-through rate is too low, Google suspends the ad or places it lower on the page even if it outbid other ads. Ads clicked on frequently are assumed to be relevant and not likely to bother users. By clicking or not clicking, users decide what ads appear. Clever, indeed, but does it work?

In 2001, at a time when most dot-coms were closing their doors, Google earned a profit of $7 million, and in 2002 $100 million. Pay-per-click advertising worked.

In 2004, the privately-owned company arranged for an initial public offering (IPO) of shares. Taking their company public[5] was a frightening prospect for Brin and Page. It would raise lots of cash, but it also meant competing companies could see how profitable Google had become, and shareholders might have the power to change the company's goals. On August 19, 2004, Google went public, offering 19,605,052 of its 270 million shares at $85 per share on the NASDAQ stock exchange. At the end of the first day of trading, over 22 million shares changed hands, with the shares valued at $100.34. Google now had a market capitalization[6] of $23 billion dollars.

At the close of 2006, the stock market value of Google ranked third among U.S. corporations, trailing only Microsoft and Wal-Mart. Google continues to expand its services to achieve its goal of making all the information in the world available online. Google Book Search, for example, aims to have searchable versions of millions of books online, including rare books from university library collections. Google Earth offers up-close satellite photographs of the entire planet. To expand its click-through advertising income, Google has made deals to provide search and advertising for Time Warner's America Online and New Corp.'s popular MySpace. And in October 2006 Google announced its purchase of YouTube, the popular online video site, for $1.65 billion.

Is Google a bubble? Can it keep growing and generate enough sales to justify the high price of its shares (nearly 60 times its earnings to close 2006)? So far Google is financially sound[7]. In 2005, Google owed no money, had profits of $1.5 billion on sales of $6.1 billion while holding $2.5 billion in cash—numbers that suggest that Google can expand without taking on debt. Larry Page and Sergey Brin are no doubt brilliant and innovative, but the odds say they will eventually make mistakes, and other bright people may figure out a way to cut into their search engine business. Plus, as a company grows, its talent becomes diluted[8]. Has Google already captured so much of the Internet search and advertising market that it will now have to expand into areas where Google's brilliant team has less expertise?

If you want to follow the ongoing Google story, it is simple. Just type "goog" into Google's search engine to see how its stock is doing.

---

[4] *click-through rate*: the number of times users click on an ad
[5] *take a company public*: make it possible for the general public to buy shares in the company. Each share represents ownership of a small piece of the company, which allows shareholders to influence company policies.
[6] *market capitalization*: the number of shares in existence multiplied by the value of those shares. On February 27, 2007, Google, Inc. had a "market cap" of $137.39 billion ($448.77 × 306.16 million shares). This number is a measure of a company's success.
[7] *sound*: healthy
[8] *dilute*: weaken by spreading thin

READING COMPREHENSION

A. Mark each sentence as *T* (true) or *F* (false) according to the information in Reading 1. Use the dictionary to help you understand new words.

.... 1. Larry Page and Sergey Brin studied the behavior of pigeons to design their search engine.

.... 2. Page and Brin stayed ahead of competitors and tricksters by regularly modifying their search engine.

.... 3. The reading implies that Yahoo made a mistake when it did not buy Google for $1 million.

.... 4. Google results pages give priority to advertisers over other types of results.

.... 5. Google makes its money by loading every search results page with advertising.

.... 6. Google is no longer a privately held company.

.... 7. Google would like to make it possible for users to read many different kinds of books online.

.... 8. The reading predicts that Google will soon face financial problems.

B. Imagine that you need to check some information in Reading 1 for a report. Scan the article quickly to find answers to these questions. First think about the words you will scan for.

1. Where did the two founders of Google get started on their project?

2. What word did the reading use to describe the way the Google search engine works?

3. In what year was Google founded?

4. Did Google lose money during the years when the dot-com bubble burst?

5. What does IPO stand for?

6. Did Google have a lot of debts at the time the article was written?

READING STRATEGY: Analyzing Criteria

A criterion is a condition or description used when making judgments. We establish criteria (plural) so that we can be consistent and accurate. Reading 1 gives evidence that Google is a successful company. We know this because Google meets many criteria for success:

- It has millions of customers and a well-known trademark.
- It has a successful product that the current competition cannot beat.
- It generates billions of dollars of revenue.
- It is financially sound with no debt and lots of cash.
- It has a high market capitalization.

A. Let's consider the long-term survival of Google. Read these criteria that indicate whether a company is likely to survive and grow. Skim Reading 1 and identify which criteria Google meets by answering the questions. Write *Yes*, *No*, or *?* (if you're not sure).

.... **1.** customers and market share: *Does the company have a large customer base?*

.... **2.** market capitalization: *If the company is publicly traded, does its stock have a high value?*

.... **3.** business model: *Does the company have a business model that will lead to profit?*

.... **4.** growth: *Does the company have a potential for growth in its core business?*

.... **5.** expansion: *Can the company expand into new markets either through developing new products or acquiring existing ones?*

.... **6.** liquidity: *Does the company have enough cash to fund current and future operations?*

.... **7.** debt: *Does the company have a manageable amount of debt?*

.... **8.** competitive advantage: *Is it difficult for other companies to imitate this company?*

.... **9.** trademark: *Does the company have a recognized name or logo?*

.... **10.** management: *Can the company survive changes in management?*

.... **11.** talent: *Can the company hold onto its talent or attract new talent?*

B. Do you think Google meets enough criteria to continue its success into the future? Discuss your ideas in a small group.

VOCABULARY ACTIVITIES

Noun	Verb	Adjective	Adverb
bias	bias	biased unbiased	....
computer computation	compute	computational computed	computationally
constant	....	constant	constantly
editor edition editorial	edit	edited editorial	....
formula	formulate	formulaic	formulaically
founder	found	founded unfounded	....
relevance	....	relevant irrelevant	relevantly

A. Fill in the blanks with a target word from the chart that completes the sentence in a grammatical and meaningful way. Be sure to use the correct form.

1. Many dot-coms in the late 1990s were .... on an unsound business model.

2. The business was under .... pressure to expand into new markets.

3. A complicated algorithm .... the importance of each web page for the purposes of ranking it.

4. What is Google's .... for success?

5. I know he's a hard worker and wants the job, but unfortunately that's not really .... We need someone with real expertise in the field.

6. The websites of many reputable newspapers lack the careful .... of the print editions. They are full of errors.

B. The word *bias* has technical and non-technical uses. Which meaning of the word *bias* is expressed in each sentence? Match the sentence on the left with the definition on the right. Compare answers with a partner.

.... 1. Since the defendant was a relative, the judge recused himself to avoid any charges of bias.

.... 2. The results of the research are biased because they did not include a broad enough sample of students.

.... 3. The course covers world history, but with a bias toward the Renaissance.

.... 4. Brin and Page's solution allows ads but does not bias the page ranking results in favor of advertisers.

.... 5. She assured both sides that she had nothing at stake in the outcome and was trained to make an unbiased judgment.

a. favoritism toward one side in an argument, decision, or report

b. actions or attitudes favoring one group over another

c. favoring or focusing on one aspect of a broad subject

d. not favoring one side or the other

e. having an error in a statistical study

C. Here are some studies where the sample may be biased. What bias can you detect in the sampling method? Discuss your ideas with a partner.

1. Researchers want to know which candidate for public office is more popular. So they call people's homes Monday morning, one day before the election. Candidate A is more popular in the telephone study, but Candidate B wins Tuesday's election easily. What happened?

2. Researchers wonder if cold winter weather might reduce arthritis pain, the leading cause of disability for people over 55. So they compare sales of arthritis pain medicine during the winter in Utah, a cold state, and Florida, a warmer state. A sampling of pharmacies showed higher arthritis pain medication sales in Florida. Should we trust the results of this study?

We can raise doubts about a claim if we show that the arguments and evidence offered in support are *irrelevant*. Consider the analogy used to support the thesis "university education should be free."

Analogy   Both education and air are necessary for a successful life. Air is free, so university education should be free, too.

Most people agree that education and air are necessary, but the argument is weak because the similarity is irrelevant. Air is free because it is plentiful, not because it is necessary. There are also degrees of necessity. To be convincing, an analogy needs many *relevant* similarities and few *relevant* differences.

D. Analogies are used to support each of these theses. Are the similarities relevant? Can you think of any relevant differences? Discuss your answers in a small group.

1. Thesis: Parents should have to get a license before they have children.

   Argument: A poorly raised child can do as much damage as an unlicensed driver of a motor vehicle. Citizens are required to pass a driving exam before driving a car alone. Likewise, parents should be required to prove they are competent parents before they are permitted to have a child.

2. Thesis: Children should not be required to go to school.

   Argument: Forcing children to attend school is a violation of their rights. Students and prisoners both must remain in a facility against their will for extended periods of time. Prisoners can't be put in prison unless convicted in a court of law. Children are forced to go school without a trial. Therefore, forcing children to go to school is a form of illegal imprisonment.

3. Thesis: Smoking should be allowed on public sidewalks in the downtown areas of major cities.

   Argument: People can eat and drink while they're walking on the sidewalk, so they should be able to smoke, too.

BEFORE YOU READ

Read these questions. Discuss your answers in small groups.

1. Successful companies, like Google, tend to attract suspicion and the attention of *watchdogs*—people or groups who monitor their activities. What kind of things might these watchdogs look for?

2. Internet companies can collect information on the interests and purchasing habits of Internet users by examining the kinds of sites they visit. Is this an invasion of privacy? Should companies limit the kind of information they collect?

3. Are governments justified in censoring the content that citizens can access on the Internet? If so, what content should governments censor?

MORE WORDS YOU'LL NEED

copyright: the legal right given to the originator of a "work" to publish or print it in any form and to prevent others from copying it or publishing it illegally

fraud: the act of cheating or deceiving someone in some way (the adjective is *fraudulent*)

a royalty: a sum of money paid to an author or composer for each copy of a work sold or performed

READ

This article discusses some of the challenges faced by Google when its business model came into conflict with reality.

Google Controversies

When Google founders Larry Page and Sergey Brin began their quest for the perfect search engine at Stanford University in the mid 1990s, they had a lofty[1] goal—to make all
5 the information in the world available online for free. Within a few years, they had achieved much of that goal and were able to bring vast amounts of information to anyone with access to the Internet. "Google it" is now a common
10 phrase in many of the world's languages.

Google has an unusual company motto: *Don't be evil.* Most people familiar with Page and Brin's achievements would likely agree that the two have improved the world and lived up to
15 that motto. But Google's astounding rise from a start-up company working out of a garage to one of the most recognized brand names in the world has naturally attracted scrutiny[2]. And there are many who have raised questions about
20 the ethics and legality of Google's business practices.

One complaint is "click fraud." Advertisers make bids to place ads along the top and right hand sides of Google search result pages.
25 When **potential** customers click on an ad, Google collects a fee ranging from a few pennies to $30 or more, depending on how high the bidding went. Advertisers worry that

[1] *lofty*: noble
[2] *scrutiny*: close inspection

dishonest businesses click on a competitor's ad
30 to drive up their advertising costs. Non-Google
websites can also cheat advertisers. To extend
its advertising reach, Google allows websites
to display Google ads and earn a fee when the
ads are clicked on. Google prohibits website
35 owners from clicking on an ad they host, but
there is still room for mischief if a website
owner uses different IP addresses[3] to make
fraudulent clicks. Google assures advertisers
that it has sophisticated software that identifies
40 fraudulent clicks and removes them before they
are charged to the advertiser, but critics contend
that Google has not made a big enough effort to
police click fraud and has little incentive to do
so since Google profits from fraudulent clicks.
45 Advertisers are particularly frustrated over
the difficulty of proving click fraud. Without
greater policing, the problem may solve itself.
Advertisers may punish Google by bidding lower
in order to **offset** losses due to click fraud.

50   The most complicated issue from a legal
standpoint is copyright law. In the United
States, for example, any book published
after 1923 is protected by copyright laws.
Printing and **distributing** copies of the work
55 requires permission of the copyright owner,
and copyright owners often demand a royalty
payment. Google Book Search and the Google
Library Project aim to digitize millions of books
and host them online in a searchable **format**.
60 The value of such an enterprise is undisputed.
Scholars will have easy access to rare books.
Many authors believe Google Book Search will
provide free publicity and a new avenue for
sales. But others worry that Google will use
65 their works without paying royalties. Google
has addressed this fear by touting Book Search
as a book marketing program, where authors
sell their works, not an online library. Google
also allows authors to remove their books from

70 Google Book Search if they wish. Despite these
reassurances, we can expect Google to face
many legal challenges in the coming years from
authors and publishers. Google's acquisition in
October 2006 of YouTube, the popular Internet
75 video download site, also involves unresolved
copyright issues that should keep courts busy in
the United States and around the world.
    Google's services have raised several privacy
issues. Gmail, Google's free email service,
80 supports itself by inserting ads into emails
that Gmail account holders receive. If the user
clicks on the ad, Google collects a fee from the
advertiser. Privacy is an issue because of the
way Google chooses the ads. To target the ads
85 toward the interests of the user, Google reads
the content of incoming email to search for
keywords that will trigger the ads. If these were
generic ads placed in all emails automatically, few
would complain. But scanning content strikes
90 some as an invasion of privacy. Google defends
the practice by saying that the emails are only
read by computers, not people, for the purpose
of ad placement and that many email services do
the same thing in order to detect spam[4]. Critics,
95 however, feel Google should not analyze the
email from non-Gmail accounts unless it gets
the sender's permission first. They also worry
that Google's email records could be used by
governments to spy on private communication.
100   The fear of government intrusion extends
to other aspects of Google's operation. Google
has huge data collections that could be seized
by governments and analyzed at relatively
little cost. In the past, collecting data on,
105 let's say, people who had read or purchased a
controversial book would require an army of
investigators to search through library records
and bookstore sales. It is hard to imagine a
government even bothering. But data mining[5]
110 through a single database could quickly yield

---

[3] *IP address*: Internet Protocol Address; a computer address used to identify devices using the Internet, such as
Internet Service Providers and printers. It can be compared to a telephone number in a phone network.
[4] *spam*: undesired email sent in bulk or irrelevant messages posted on a forum or blog (web log)
[5] *data mining*: electronically searching huge databases for small pieces of relevant information, such as a list of
customers who buy a specific product

leads if Google has access to library records and has copies of emails sent between online booksellers and customers.

As Google extends the **scope** of its operations overseas, questions concerning freedom of speech have arisen. In its early days, Google saw itself as operating outside of government control and offering an unrestricted resource for finding information. But Google's relationship with the Chinese government causes many to feel Google has compromised its independence from government intrusion. In order to offer its web services within China, Google had to make a tough decision: accept certain restrictions imposed by the Chinese government or risk losing out on the Chinese market. For the first time, Google faced a decision with major political implications and felt pressure to **clarify** the meaning of their noble "Don't be evil" principle. As CEO Eric Schmidt tells it, Google used an "evil scale" to weigh its decision. Living with the Chinese government's restrictions is less evil than not serving Chinese users at all. And less profitable, critics might add. Google's decision led to bad press[6] around the world and requests for hearings in the U.S. Congress.

Despite these legal and ethical issues, Google remains an extremely popular company. After all, its most popular products are free. But it is also an aggressive company with big goals, a company that likes surprises and challenges. Many observers feel it is ready for a showdown[7] with software giant Microsoft over who will control the next generation of personal computing. Others worry that Google will impede development of the Internet. Right now it dominates Web 2.0, a nickname for the current Internet. The fear is that Google will use its power to prevent Web 3.0 by blocking improvements that might threaten its dominance. Can Google win and stay on top without playing dirty and tarnishing its image as the Internet good guy?

---

[6] *bad press*: negative news reports
[7] *showdown*: confrontation between two rivals to settle an argument

READING COMPREHENSION

Mark each sentence as *T* (true) or *F* (false) according to the information in Reading 2. Use the dictionary to help you understand new words.

.... 1. Some critics feel that Google's effort to dominate the Internet has compromised its company motto.

.... 2. Google has refused to do anything to combat click fraud.

.... 3. In the coming years, we can expect many battles in court involving the Internet and intellectual property.

.... 4. Gmail promises not to scan the content of individual emails.

.... 5. Data mining raises privacy issues for many Google users.

.... 6. The reading claims that Google's goal is to prevent other companies from improving Internet services.

READING STRATEGY: Determining Degree

Earlier in this unit, you evaluated Google's potential by asking whether the company met several criteria important for growth. You were asked to answer the questions with a *yes* or *no*. Most of the answers, however, were not absolutes—definitely yes or definitely no. Rather, they could distribute themselves along a continuum between yes and no.

A. With a partner, examine these criteria and decide whether they are absolute categories (*A*) or whether the answers could distribute themselves along a continuum of values (*C*).

.... **1.** Is the company listed on a stock exchange?

.... **2.** Does it have a high market capitalization?

.... **3.** Is it a non-profit corporation?

.... **4.** Does it have an experienced top management?

.... **5.** Does the company have potential for earnings growth?

B. There are several ways to use a continuum. One popular format asks people to indicate agreement or disagreement with a statement on a 5-point scale. Based on what you read in Reading 2, how would you rate Google's ethics? Discuss your answer in a small group.

Google's business practices are ethical.

.... **1.** Strongly disagree .... **2.** Disagree .... **3.** Neither agree nor disagree .... **4.** Agree .... **5.** Strongly agree

C. You can also determine the degree of relevance or importance by ranking criteria. Drawing on what you read in Reading 2, first decide on four more criteria that could be used to judge whether a company is ethical. Then, rank each criterion's importance, with *1* as highest and *5* as lowest.

.... *Are the company's products and services typically used to cheat people?*

....

....

....

....

D. CEO Eric Schmidt says that Google uses an "evil scale" to weigh its decisions and determine its business practices. His scale apparently involves choosing the lesser evil. What criteria would you use to decide if a business practice is evil? How would you rank the criteria?

VOCABULARY ACTIVITIES

Noun	Verb	Adjective	Adverb
clarification	clarify	clarified	....
distribution distributor	distribute	distributive	....
format	format	formatted unformatted	....
investigator investigation	investigate	investigative	....
....	offset	offset offsetting	....
potential potentiality	....	potential	potentially
scope	scope (out)	....	....

A. Fill in the blank with a target word from the chart above that completes the sentence in a grammatical and meaningful way. Be sure to use the correct form.

1. In response to a query, search engines have the .... to search every book, paper, or article ever published.

2. Google has used the same basic .... for its home page since its inception. It has no graphics except the Google logo and limits text to just over 40 words.

3. If a web page uses Google ads, a portion of the advertising fee is .... to the web page owner.

4. Since its initial appearance, Google has expanded the .... of it operation to include dozens of services and products.

5. In early 2006, Google's operations in China prompted members of the U.S. Congress to call for a(n) ....

6. Critics have called on Google, Yahoo, and other companies to .... their company policies concerning search engine censorship.

Collocations Chart

Verb/Adverb	Adjective	Noun	Verb/Prepositional Phrase
seek, demand, request, ask for	further	*clarification*	of sth
clarify	....	meaning, intention, position, point, issue, situation	....
....	*constant*	use, need, pressure, complaint, problem, supply, reminder	....
....	fixed, standard, new, different, useful, typical, accessible, traditional	*format*	....
formulate	....	policy, response, solution, idea, strategy, proposal, plan	....
....	*investigative*	report, journalist, procedures, team	....
attach, see, hold, have, find	little, no, considerable, increasing, decreasing, declining, obvious, direct, special, particular	*relevance*	....
expand, extend, broaden, match, reduce, limit, restrict, define, determine	....	(the) *scope*	of the problem, law, program, book, course, plan, work, study

B. The chart above shows some of the more predictable collocations, or word partners, for selected target vocabulary. Using the chart, complete these sentences with a likely word. Be sure to use the correct form.

1. The .... team uncovered evidence of widespread ethical violations.

2. They decided to restrict the .... of their study to smaller companies with a market capitalization under $50 million.

3. The management was under .... pressure to cut payroll.

4. The press pressured the CEO to .... the meaning of his company's recent announcement.

5. The CEO's statement seemed to have little or no .... to the issues raised during the investigation.

6. The portable listening device used files of a different .... from those used by other devices on the market.

7. We will need to seek further .... of this matter before making a decision.

8. The committee met and .... a new strategy for expanding into overseas markets.

C. *Distribute* and *distribution* have the general meaning of giving something out or spreading something in an organized way. Which meaning of *distribute* is expressed in the sentences? Match the sentences on the left with the definitions on the right. Compare answers with a partner.

.... 1. Each year a portion of the company's profits were distributed to the employees as a year-end bonus.

a. give out items widely to a group

.... 2. To distribute weight better throughout the plane, the flight attendant invited several passengers to sit in First Class.

b. the act of supplying goods to retailers to sell

.... 3. This year the business extended the distribution of its cheese products to North America for the first time.

c. spread something evenly throughout a system

.... 4. Several countries have been accused of permitting businesses to distribute copyrighted works without paying royalties.

d. the location of something across a wide area

.... 5. The diagram shows the distribution of the animal populations in this area.

e. divide something into portions and give it out

D. Build sentences using a random generator: Your teacher or partner calls out a random two-digit number to identify two words from the lists below. You then use those words to write a grammatical and meaningful sentence.

Teacher: "2-1." [The two words are "constant" (2) and "distribution" (1).]

Possible sentence: "Our company's distribution network has constant delays."

0. bias
1. clarify
2. constant
3. edit
4. founded
5. potential
6. offset
7. irrelevant
8. unbiased
9. relevance

0. compute
1. distribution
2. format
3. formula
4. investigate
5. scope
6. formulate
7. distribute
8. unfounded
9. investigation

WRITING AND DISCUSSION TOPICS

1. Other companies, institutions, and individuals besides Google have developed or are developing innovative ideas important for the Internet. Research one of these topics and describe the nature of the innovation and why it is significant in the history or future of the Internet.

WebCrawler	wikis	Arpanet and packet switching
Killer applications	Web 2.0	folksonomy
Gopher	Ebay	Web 3.0
Mosaic	PayPal	semantic web

2. Choose one of these questions and develop a list of criteria that will help answer it. Do all of the criteria have to be met or just one? Present your ideas to the class.

   - What criteria can we use to decide if someone is a good parent?
   - What criteria can we use to decide if a business practice is unethical?
   - What criteria can we use to decide if someone is an effective teacher?
   - What criteria can we use to decide if someone has leadership ability?
   - What criteria can we use to decide if someone has artistic talent?

3. Copyright infringement is a growing international controversy. On the one hand, we want those who produce creative works to receive payment for their work. If not, the incentive to produce innovative works may diminish. On other the hand, we want the Internet to offer easy, low-cost access to sources of information and entertainment. Is it possible to do both? Discuss possible ways to resolve this controversy.

MODELING NATURE

In this unit, you will

- ⮕ read about how the field of robotics is using models in nature to create machines.
- ⮕ learn about analyzing advantages and disadvantages.
- ⮕ increase your understanding of the target academic words for this unit:

bulk	comprise	furthermore	notion	schedule
capacity	consist	illustrate	proceed	shift
code	document	method	project	

SELF-ASSESSMENT OF TARGET WORDS

Think carefully about how well you know each target word in this unit. Then, write it in the appropriate column in the chart. When you've finished this unit, come back and reassess your knowledge of the target words.

I have never seen the word before.	I have seen the word but am not sure what it means.	I understand the word when I see or hear it in a sentence.	I have tried to use the word, but I am not sure I am using it correctly.	I use the word with confidence in either speaking *or* writing.	I use the word with confidence, both in speaking *and* writing.

BEFORE YOU READ

Read these questions. Discuss your answers in small groups.

1. Imagine that you are a traveling salesperson and you have to travel to the towns represented on the map below. You want to find the shortest route that will take you to every town once. What strategy would you use to decide on a route? Here are some possibilities you might consider.

   • Find a route where you do not retrace your steps and assume it is good enough.

   • Always travel to the nearest town that you have not visited yet.

   • Measure each likely route.

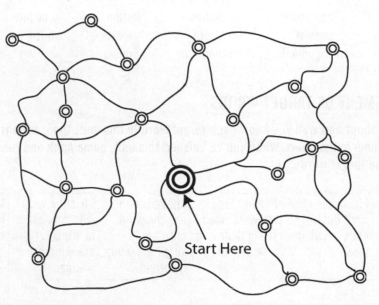

Start Here

2. Whatever method you used to find an acceptable route, you had the advantage of being able to look ahead. What strategy would you use if you had to ask directions in each town and, thus, could only see one town ahead? What question would you ask?

3. What household tasks or chores can you imagine robots doing in the near future?

MORE WORDS YOU'LL NEED

allocate: distribute something for a particular purpose in an organized way

feasible: possible to do easily or practically

forage: search for food, usually over a wide area

logistical: relating to the detailed organization of a complex operation that involves a lot of people and equipment

optimize: make the best use of something; use something in an efficient or perfect way

Biologists have learned a lot about the behavior of ants. This knowledge, it turns out, has surprising implications for robot design.

The Swarm Bots Are Coming

Ant algorithms get down to business

Ants are simple creatures, yet they can perform complicated tasks. They create highways leading to food, organize the distribution of larvae[1] in the anthill, form cemeteries by clustering dead
5 ants, build living bridges to cross gaps in their way, and assign and **shift** tasks as needed without any centralized control. Thus, ants provide an excellent **illustration** of how simple devices can achieve complex results.

10 Boil down ant behavior and what do you get? A new set of business tools known as ant algorithms: basic behaviors that can be programmed into a large number of independent software agents to solve human problems.

15 Consider the way ants forage. When an ant comes across food, it returns to the nest, leaving a scent trail. Other ants follow the trail, find the goods, and carry them back to the nest, reinforcing the path with their own scent, which
20 attracts still more ants. Shorter routes get more traffic, so the scent becomes stronger along these, while it dies away on longer, lesser-used ones. Using this **method**, ants follow the shortest paths between their nest and nearby food sources.

25 This route-finding capability is remarkably handy. Colonies of simulated ants laying down digital scent trails can find the best way to send delivery trucks through city streets or data packets through communication networks.
30 More generally, ant algorithms can find minimum-cost solutions to a variety of logistical problems in distribution and **scheduling**. Unilever uses them to allocate storage tanks, chemical mixers, and packaging facilities.
35 Southwest Airlines uses them to optimize its cargo operations. Numerous consulting

houses, such as the Swiss firm AntOptima, have embraced them as an indispensable tool.

But logistics are just the beginning. Ant
40 algorithms are also being used to control a class of robots called swarm bots. Typically, a swarm bot is a collection of simple robots (s-bots) that self-organize according to algorithms inspired by the bridge-building and task-allocation activities
45 of ants. For example, if an s-bot encounters an object too heavy or **bulky** to carry on its own, other s-bots will grasp either the object or other s-bots until they get it under control. Two or more can link up to cross a gap that
50 exceeds a single s-bot's stride. With this ability to temporarily mass together or spread out, a swarm bot's form depends on its surroundings and the job it's doing. Such devices might prove helpful in activities like search-and-rescue and
55 planetary exploration.

Swarm bots helping each other up a step

The ability to swarm, adapt, and optimize—all the skills implied by ant behavior—makes ant algorithms a crucial technology for the information age, especially as everyday objects
60 become ever smarter. The rules that insects live by turn out to be perfectly suited to the high-tech anthill.

---

[1] Insects go through three stages of development—egg, larva, and pupa (pl. = larvae and pupae)

Bye Swarm Bots, Hello Swarmanoids

Move over swarm bots, the swarmanoid is coming.

A team at the Free University of Brussels in Belgium is embarking on a 42-month research **project** to build and test a 60-strong swarm of small, autonomous[2] robots — the swarmanoid — capable of collaborating in 3-D environments.

The swarmanoid initiative follows the successful completion of the swarm-bots project, in which the researchers demonstrated the ability of identical robots to work in formations to overcome challenges such as carrying heavy objects and traveling across rough terrain — tasks that a single swarm bot could not accomplish alone.

The $3.5 million project will feature footbots, handbots, and eyebots, said Marco Dorigo, research director at the university's IRIDIA lab.

The three types of bots will join forces to create a swarmanoid and perform various jobs. The footbots will transport objects on the ground level, while handbots with specialized climbing and grappling[3] devices take to the walls. Some eyebots equipped with visual sensors will operate attached to the ceiling, overseeing the action below and feeding information to their robotic colleagues; others will fly.

"The long-term vision is to build robots that, like humanoid robots, are supposed to live in human-made environments," Dorigo said. "But instead of the anthropomorphic[4] vision of humans in robots, we want to take the swarm approach."

The swarmanoid's footbot design will be based on the swarm-bot architecture. But the scientists decided the bots would be more practical if different models were customized for particular jobs.

"Why try to solve problems using a single type when you can have robots that are specialized for specific tasks?" he said. To demonstrate the swarmanoid's abilities, the team wants to create a swarmanoid that can tidy a bedroom, as well as remove an object from a shelf and bring it to a humanoid.

In the long term, a swarmanoid could be used in earthquake rescue situations, or perform specialized tasks in buildings and factories. Dorigo said he hopes to publish his work in late 2007, and to have experimental results in about two years.

Other robotics experts agree that various types of robots working together will be the most useful.

"For robotics to really make an impact in the world, we have to get lots of robots into people's hands," said Tucker Balch, associate professor in interactive and intelligent computing at the Georgia Institute of Technology, who works in multi-robot team research.

"The two barriers to that are cost and utility, but it becomes feasible with the swarm idea, which would allow households to buy several inexpensive robots that could work together," Balch said. "The view of swarms **consisting** of all identical robots just isn't going to take off."

The use of different kinds of robots in the same team follows the division of labor in ant colonies extremely well, said Payman Arabshahi, of the University of Washington's Applied Physics Lab. **Furthermore**, if scientists can scale the robots to a much smaller size than an ant, the possibilities are endless.

---

[2] *autonomous*: able to operate independently as a separate entity. An *automaton* is a machine or process that can perform tasks automatically without an operator.

[3] *grappling*: relating to features that will allow them to hook or attach themselves to the walls in order to climb

[4] *anthropomorphic*: attributing human characteristics to an animal or object

135 "It's not too far-fetched[5] to think that if we take the concept of self-assembling robots to the micro or even nano[6] level, you could have cases where micro-robots would self-assemble inside the human body for a certain procedure and 140 then disassemble and essentially self-destruct after the procedure is done," said Arabshahi.

---

[5] *far-fetched*: improbable
[6] *nano-*: prefix meaning extremely small; usually used to describe technical or mechanical things. Nanotechnology, for example, aims to invent microscopic machines, perhaps at the molecular level.

READING COMPREHENSION

A. Mark each sentence as T (true) or F (false) according to the information in Reading 1. Use the dictionary to help you understand new words.

.... 1. Ants respond to instructions communicated from the center of the nest.

.... 2. As the strength of a scent trail diminishes, ants show less interest in that path.

.... 3. Ant algorithms are currently being used to assist in search and rescue operations.

.... 4. Swarm bots and swarmanoids do not bear much resemblance to humans.

.... 5. Swarmanoids will mostly be confined to industrial uses.

.... 6. Tucker Balch sees little consumer demand for swarms of identical robots carrying out household tasks.

.... 7. Developers envision a day when robots will perform medical operations on humans.

B. Scan the reading to find the sentences paraphrased below. Write the line number in the blank.

.... 1. Ants show us how complex problems can be solved by tiny machines following simple instructions.

.... 2. And then there is the way that ants find and retrieve food.

.... 3. There are many amazing uses for this ability to find their way from one point to another.

.... 4. Designing robots with different skills to work as a team seems the most promising approach.

.... 5. Right now robots are too expensive for home use and would not be really useful or practical. However, ...

READING STRATEGY: Analyzing Advantages and Disadvantages

Reading assignments may ask you to weigh the advantages and disadvantages of an idea or plan. Reading 1, for example, might prompt these questions:

- What benefits can we gain from studying ant algorithms?
- What advantages do swarm bots have?
- What is one drawback of using teams of identical swarm bots?
- What problems are solved by using swarmanoids?

A. Read these lists of potential advantages and disadvantages that might be relevant when analyzing a plan or idea. Can you think of other considerations to add to each list?

Advantages	Disadvantages
inexpensive	expensive
efficient	wasteful, inefficient
simple to understand	complicated
convenient, easy to use	takes too long to design or build
quick to install, operate, or replace	dangerous
easy to modify or expand	fragile; needs frequent replacement
safe and reliable	expensive to clean, maintain, or repair
durable	dangerous, risky
easy to clean, maintain, and repair	dirty and polluting
widely available	limited availability
....	....
....	....
....	....

B. Drawing on information from the readings, list advantages and disadvantages for each of these technological solutions. The readings may imply advantages and disadvantages not directly discussed.

	Advantages	Disadvantages
ant algorithms		
swarm bots		
anthropomorphic robots		
swarmanoids		

VOCABULARY ACTIVITIES

Noun	Verb	Adjective	Adverb/Conjunction
bulk bulkiness	....	bulky bulk	....
....	consist (of)	....	....
....	....	....	furthermore
illustration illustrator	illustrate	illustrated illustrative	illustratively
method methodology	....	methodical	methodically
project	.....................*	....	....
schedule	schedule	scheduled scheduling	....
shift	shift	....	....

*The verb *project* and its forms arc treated in Unit 4.

A. Read this article on Mars mini-probes, a possible application of swarm technology. Fill in the blanks with a target word from the chart above that completes the sentence in a grammatical and meaningful way. Be sure to use the correct form.

The effort over the last 40 years to explore the planet Mars with robots has had mixed success. Some researchers believe it's time for us to (1) .... our thinking away from rolling robots of the *Star Wars* R2-D2 type.

One alternative being explored at the Massachusetts Institute of Technology (MIT) is the feasibility of sending a team of swarming robots that (2) .... spread out over the planet in every direction. Previous Mars rovers were too heavy and (3) .... to explore the nooks and crannies of Mars without risking destruction. The proposed robot team would (4) .... of hundreds or even thousands of tennis-ball-sized robots designed to hop, bounce, or roll across the rugged terrain of Mars. Each probe will have its own fuel cell and carry different kinds of sensors to collect scientific samples.

With funding from the National Aeronautics and Space Administration of the United States, the (5) .... can now proceed from the concept stage to the prototype stage. The current (6) .... calls for thc probes to be ready for a mission to Mars by about 2017.

B. The words in bold have more than one meaning, depending on context. Read these sentences and circle the meaning that best fits the context.

1. They **shifted** their attention to the problem of the mini-probe's fuel supply.

   a. changed focus   **b.** changed position

2. The **bulk** of the meeting was devoted to logistics and scheduling.

   a. majority   **b.** large size

3. The project was under budget and ahead of **schedule**.

   a. a timeline of tasks to complete   **b.** a table of prices or rates

4. The poll detected a significant **shift** in public opinion.

   a. a work period   **b.** a change in attitude

5. The company buys its paper products in **bulk**.

   a. large sizes   **b.** large, unpackaged quantities

6. You will find the cost **schedule** on an insert at the back of the catalogue.

   a. a timeline of tasks to complete   **b.** a table of prices or rates

7. The article clearly **illustrates** why there is growing interest in swarm technology.

   a. provides pictures showing   **b.** provides examples showing

READING 2

BEFORE YOU READ

Read these questions. Discuss your answers in small groups.

1. Are robots with humanlike intelligence a development that we should embrace or fear?

2. What characteristics or qualities must a machine have in order to be considered a robot?

MORE WORDS YOU'LL NEED

aspiration: a strong desire to do something, a hope or ambition

emulate: try to be like something else; design or create an artificial copy that looks and behaves the same as the original

Our ancient quest to create androids is about to destroy the boundary between humans and machines. Futurist, author and inventor Ray Kurzweil explains how and ponders the implications.

Robots 'R' Us

Human experience is marked by a refusal to obey our limitations. We've escaped the ground, we've escaped the planet, and now, after thousands of years of effort, our quest to build
5 machines that emulate our own appearance, movement, and intelligence is leading us to the point where we will escape the two most fundamental confines of all: our bodies and our minds. Once this point comes—once the
10 accelerating pace of technological change allows us to build machines that not only equal but surpass human intelligence—we'll see cyborgs (machine-enhanced humans), androids (human-robot hybrids), and other combinations beyond
15 what we can even imagine.

Although the ancient Greeks were among the first to build machines that could emulate the intelligence and natural movements of people, these efforts flowered in the European
20 Renaissance, which produced the first androids with lifelike movements. These included a mandolin-playing lady, constructed in 1540 by Italian inventor Gianello Torriano. In 1772 Swiss watchmaker Pierre Jacquet-Droz built a pensive
25 child named L'Écrivain (The Writer) that could write passages with a pen. L'Écrivain's brain was a mechanical computer that was impressive for its complexity even by today's standards.

Such inventions led scientists and
30 philosophers to speculate that the human brain itself was just an elaborate automaton. Around 1700 Wilhelm Leibniz wrote, "What if these theories are really true, and we were magically shrunk and put into someone's brain while
35 he was thinking. We would see all the pumps, pistons, gears, and levers working away, and

we would be able to **document** their workings completely, in mechanical terms, thereby completely describing the thought processes of
40 the brain. But that description would nowhere contain any mention of thought! It would consist of nothing but descriptions of pumps, pistons, levers!"

Leibniz was on to something. There are
45 indeed pumps, pistons, and levers inside our brain—we now recognize them as neurotransmitters, ion channels,[1] and the other molecular components of the neural machinery. And although we don't yet fully understand
50 the details of how these little machines create thought, our ignorance won't last much longer.

The word "robot" originated almost a century ago. Czech dramatist Karel Capek first used the term in his 1921 play R.U.R. (for "Rossum's
55 Universal Robots"), creating it from the Czech word "robota," meaning obligatory work. In the play, he describes the invention of intelligent biomechanical machines intended as servants for their human creators. While lacking charm
60 and goodwill, his robots brought together all the elements of machine intelligence: vision, touch sensitivity, pattern recognition, decision-making, world knowledge, fine motor coordination, and even a measure of common sense.

65 Capek intended his intelligent machines to be evil in their perfect rationality and scornful of human frailty. These robots ultimately rise up against their masters and destroy all humankind, a dystopian[2] **notion** that has been echoed in
70 much science fiction since.

The specter[3] of machine intelligence enslaving its creators has continued to impress itself on the public consciousness. But more significantly,

---

[1] *ion channels*: chemicals that transmit electrical signals between cells in the brain and proteins that are important for controlling the flow of electrical energy in cells
[2] *dystopian*: relating to *distopia*—a world that has gone bad, the opposite of *utopia*, or a perfect world
[3] *specter*: a haunting image

Capek's robots introduced the idea of the robot
75 as an imitation or substitute for a human being.
The idea has been reinforced throughout the
20th century, as androids engaged the popular
imagination in fiction and film, from Rosie (in
the 1960s cartoon *The Jetsons*) to C-3PO and the
80 Terminator.

The first generation of modern robots was,
however, a far cry from these anthropomorphic
visions, and most robot builders have made
no attempt to mimic humans. The Unimate, a
85 popular assembly-line robot from the 1960s,
was capable only of moving its one arm in
several directions and opening and closing its
gripper. Today, there are more than two million
Roomba robots scurrying around, performing
90 a task (vacuuming) that used to be done by
humans, but they look more like fast turtles than
housekeepers. Most robots will continue to be
utilitarian devices designed to carry out specific
tasks. But when we think of the word "robot,"
95 Capek's century-old concept of machines
made in our own image still dominates our
imagination and inspires our goals.

The aspiration to build human-level androids
can be regarded as the ultimate challenge in
100 artificial intelligence. To do it, we need to
understand not just human cognition but also
our physical skills—this is, after all, a critical part
of what the brain does. Coordinating intention
with movement in a complex environment is
105 largely the responsibility of the cerebellum,
which **comprises** more than half the neurons in
the brain. And the body itself represents much
of our complexity: There is more information in
the human genome[4], which describes the human
110 body, than in the design of the brain.

We are making tremendous strides toward
being able to understand how the brain works.
The performance/price ratio and **capacity**

of every type of information technology is
115 doubling about every year. I call this pervasive
phenomenon the law of accelerating returns. Our
grasp of biology is **proceeding** at an accelerating
pace, exponentially[5] increasing every year.
Indeed, we are augmenting and recreating nearly
120 every organ and system in the human body:
hearts and pancreases, joints and muscles.

The same progression applies to our
knowledge of the human brain. The three-
dimensional resolution[6] of brain scans has been
125 exponentially increasing, with the amount
of data that scientists are gathering on the
brain similarly increasing every year. And
they are showing that this information can be
understood by converting it into models and
130 simulations of brain regions, some two dozen of
which have already been completed.

If we are to recreate the powers of the human
brain, we first need to understand how complex
it is. There are 100 billion neurons, each with
135 thousands of connections and each connection
containing about 1,000 neural pathways.
I've estimated the amount of information
required to characterize the state of a mature
brain at thousands of trillions of bytes: a lot of
140 complexity.

But the design of the brain is a billion times
as simple as this. How do we know? The design
of the human brain—and body—is stored in the
genome, and the genome doesn't contain that
145 much information. Since we know the genome's
structure, we can compress its information to
an amount smaller than the **code** for Microsoft
Word.

My point is not that the brain is simple, but
150 that the design is at a level of complexity that
we can fathom[7] and manage. And by applying
the law of accelerating returns to the problem
of analyzing the brain's complexity, we can

---

[4] *human genome*: all of the chemical sequences encoded in human DNA
[5] *exponentially*: an extremely rapid increase, based on the idea of raising a number to the next power or exponent, e.g., 2, 4, 8, 16, 32, 64, 128, 256, etc.
[6] *resolution*: degree of clarity of an image
[7] *fathom*: comprehend

reasonably forecast that there will be exhaustive
155 models and simulations of all several hundred
regions of the human brain within about 20
years.

Once we understand how the mind operates,
we will be able to program detailed descriptions
160 of these principles into inexpensive computers,
which, by the late 2020s, will be thousands of
times as powerful as the human brain. So we will
have both the hardware and software to achieve

human-level intelligence in a machine by 2029.
165 We will also by then be able to construct fully
humanlike androids at exquisite levels of detail
and send blood cell-size robots into our bodies
and brains to keep us healthy from inside and to
augment our intellect. By the time we succeed in
170 building such machines, we will have become part
machine ourselves. We will, in other words, finally
transcend what we have so long thought of as the
ultimate limitations: our bodies and minds.

READING COMPREHENSION

A. Mark each sentence as *T* (true) or *F* (false) according to the information in Reading 2. Use the dictionary to help you understand new words.

.... **1.** Ray Kurzweil sees advanced cyborg and android robots as inevitable.

.... **2.** Karel Capek saw robots as a threat to humans.

.... **3.** According to Kurzweil, we have trouble seeing utilitarian devices as being true robots.

.... **4.** As our technological capabilities increase, technology becomes more and more expensive.

.... **5.** Kurzweil believes we have underestimated the complexity of the human brain.

.... **6.** The actual structure of the brain is less complex than the code for some computer programs.

.... **7.** According to Kurzweil, we will not only create machines with superhuman intelligence, but we will also enhance our own intelligence.

B. Scan the article for the answers to these questions. First think about the key word you will scan for. Use any annotations or highlighting you have done to help you. Compare answers with a partner.

1. What are "cyborgs" and "androids"?

2. What was "L' Écrivain" and when was it built?

3. Who was the philosopher who speculated that the brain was a mechanical system?

4. Where was Karel Capek from?

5. About how many neurons are there in the human brain?

6. About how long did Kurzweil think it would take to create an "exhaustive model" of the human brain at the time he wrote this article?

7. If Kurzweil is correct, when can we expect to see a machine with human level intelligence?

READING STRATEGY: Identifying Ethics and Values

> In weighing advantages and disadvantages, we also consider ethics, values, and morals. Will an idea or plan promote things we like or value? Will it discourage things we dislike or fear?

A. Here are some ethical and moral considerations. Can you think of others to add to the lists?

Things we want to encourage, promote, or increase		Things we want to discourage, prevent, or decrease	
good health	justice	violence	vanity
wealth	self-control	crime	laziness
freedom	trust	fatigue	dishonesty
free time/recreation	loyalty	disease	self-centeredness
taking responsibility	generosity	pain	rudeness
fairness	friendliness	poverty	irresponsible behavior
learning	politeness/civility	favoritism	immoral behavior
security	cooperation	injustice	environmental damage
beauty	bravery	greed	loss of traditions
knowledge	....	narcissism	....
amusement and fun	....	decay and ugliness	....
new experiences	....	jealousy	....

B. In approving or rejecting an idea, writers may clearly state what ethical concerns or values motivate their writing. Just as often, though, writers will imply what values are important to them. Each statement on the left describes one feature of a trend, development, or behavior. Match each statement to a desire or fear listed on the right.

.... **1.** Research shows that few people can truly function well on less than 8 hours of sleep a night.

.... **2.** Google Book Search offers free publicity and a new avenue for sales.

.... **3.** Economic bubbles make people believe that they are richer than they are.

.... **4.** Students from rural areas will be penalized.

.... **5.** A mission to Mars will increase children's interest in science and exploration.

a. It promotes curiosity and wonder.

b. It encourages irresponsible financial decision-making.

c. It encourages favoritism and unfairness.

d. It damages health.

e. It increases popularity and profits.

C. Read this comment on Kurzweil's ideas. Then, in a small group, discuss the questions that follow.

Ray Kurzweil, the author of "Robots 'R' Us," has some controversial views about the future of humans. He feels that advances in biochemistry, neurology, and computer science will allow us to redesign our bodies and our minds in ways that will make us more intelligent and perhaps immortal. Kurzweil is generally optimistic about these developments. Others may see such developments as a serious threat to our values.

1. What value is there in being able to redesign ourselves?
2. What values may be threatened by such a change?

VOCABULARY ACTIVITIES

Noun	Verb	Adjective	Adverb/Conjunction
capacity	incapacitate	incapacitated	....
code	encode decode	coded	....
....	comprise	....	....
document documentation documentary	document	(well-)documented	....
notion	....	notional	notionally
procedure proceedings proceeds	proceed (to)	procedural	procedurally

A. Fill in the blank with a target word from the chart above that completes the sentence in a grammatical and meaningful way. Be sure to use the correct form.

In many early science fiction stories, a scientist creates a robot and then the robot

(1) .... to kill its creator. But science fiction writer Isaac Asimov

disagreed with this idea. His (2) .... was that a robot could be

"sympathetic and noble." In 1940, Asimov and science fiction writer and editor John

W. Campbell conceived the Three Laws of Robotics:

*   A robot may not injure a human being or, through inaction, allow a human being to come to harm.
*   A robot must obey orders given it by human beings except where such orders would conflict with the First Law.
*   A robot must protect its own existence as long as such protection does not conflict with the First or Second Law.

continued

Three of the nine stories that (3) .... Asimov's *I, Robot* anthology mention these laws, and many of the robots in his later novels and stories follow this (4) .... of behavior.

The laws are not contained in any formal, written (5) .... that a thinking robot could refer to and quote. Instead, the laws are (6) .... mathematically into the robot's programming and operate much like the natural instinct that directs human beings to protect their own children.

For Asimov, this is analogous to safety features and strict operating (7) .... that are part of all tools and machines. But will this built-in ethical code work if machines can think for themselves? If robots develop the (8) .... for conscious thought, will they choose to ignore the three laws?

B. The words in bold have more than one meaning, depending on context. Read these sentences and circle the meaning that best fits the context.

1. The library's **capacity** is inadequate for the number of books in the collection.
   a. power to do something   **b.** amount of physical space

2. The Three Laws of Robotics are a **code** of conduct devised by science fiction writer Isaac Asimov.
   a. a secret system of letters or numbers   **b.** a set of principles

3. This **notion** was first expressed in a short story by Asimov.
   a. an idea or opinion   **b.** an impulse or desire

4. He had a sudden **notion** to call an old friend of his.
   a. an idea or opinion   **b.** an impulse or desire

5. The scientist recorded his theories in a **code** that we are just now beginning to understand.
   a. a set of principles   **b.** a secret system of letters or numbers

6. Although I don't agree with him, I'm impressed by his intellectual **capacity**.
   a. power to do something   **b.** amount of physical space

Collocations Chart

Verb	Adjective	Noun	Prepositional phrase
....	....	*bulk*	of the money, work, estate, operation, information
have	intellectual, limited, reduced, full, large, excess, creative, maximum, limitless, enormous	*capacity*	for sth
....	strict, moral, criminal, genetic, secret	*code*	of conduct, behavior, ethics, practice
....	(well-)*documented*	evidence, case, report, account, history, example, occurrences	....
have	strange, peculiar, vague, clear, false, commonplace, everyday, popular, complex	*notion*	....
adopt, follow, use, establish	simple, complex, complicated, standard, proper, correct, scientific	*procedure*	....
set up, carry out, fund, initiate	large, ambitious, worthwhile, important, joint, special	*project*	....
....	decided, definite, mental	*shift*	in emphasis, attitude, policy, perception from .... to ....
shift	....	gears, blame, burden, emphasis, cost, perspective	....

C. The chart above shows some of the more predictable collocations, or word partners, for selected target vocabulary. Using the chart, complete these sentences with a likely word. Be sure to use the correct form.

1. Many universities have a strict .... of behavior regarding plagiarism and the use of other people's intellectual property.

2. According to Ray Kurzweil, in the next 10 to 20 years, the intellectual and creative .... of computers will greatly exceed that of the human brain.

continued

3. Google has initiated an ambitious .... to digitize millions of books contained in university libraries.

4. Ant algorithms are simple decision-making .... that can solve complex problems.

5. Ray Kurzweil's prediction that humans will soon become part machine strikes many as a peculiar ....

6. Trying to understand how humans think and move is difficult because the .... of these mental operations are processed at a subconscious level.

7. So far most robot designs bear little resemblance to humans, but perhaps we will see a .... in emphasis toward more anthropomorphic robots as the processing capacity of computers greatly increases.

WRITING AND DISCUSSION TOPICS

1. Science fiction stories and movies often imagine human-like robots as either partners or villains in the future. Yet most robots today are not like humans at all. They are designed to carry out mechanical tasks that humans are not very good at or cannot do for long without risking overuse injuries. Is there any reason to develop robots that can do tasks that humans can already do well? What might those tasks be?

2. If we decide to explore space by sending an expedition to the planet Mars, do you think we should send people or robot swarms? Why?

3. In 1811, a group of workers, called Luddites, began a campaign to stop the spread of machinery in textile factories in Europe. They feared the machines would cost them their jobs. Do you think a "neo-Luddite" movement will appear if robots become more commonplace? (*neo-* means a modern version of an older concept)

4. Discuss the advantages and disadvantages of one of these futuristic proposals:
   - Implanting an electronic device in people that uniquely identifies each human being.
   - Using swarm bot "bloodhounds" to chase and locate criminals.
   - Implanting cell phone speakers and microphones inside our heads to make phone use easier.
   - Using computers, cell phone implants, and robots to educate our children.
   - Making all cars into self-driving robots.
   - Injecting bodies with swarm bots that diagnose diseases and alert us to their presence.

Unit 10

Anthropology

THE MYSTERY OF EASTER ISLAND

In this unit, you will

- ⊃ read about an amazing society that all but disappeared.
- ⊃ learn how to identify multiple causes and synthesize information from several sources.
- ⊃ increase your understanding of the target academic words for this unit:

cease	conceive	deny	quote	valid
cite	confirm	derive	supplement	widespread
collapse	culture	nevertheless	transport	

SELF-ASSESSMENT OF TARGET WORDS

Think carefully about how well you know each target word in this unit. Then, write it in the appropriate column in the chart. When you've finished this unit, come back and reassess your knowledge of the target words.

I have never seen the word before.	I have seen the word but am not sure what it means.	I understand the word when I see or hear it in a sentence.	I have tried to use the word, but I am not sure I am using it correctly.	I use the word with confidence in either speaking *or* writing.	I use the word with confidence, both in speaking *and* writing.

BEFORE YOU READ

Read this question. Discuss your answers in a small group.

In his book *Collapse*, Jared Diamond, a professor of geography at UCLA, identified eight factors within human control that have contributed to the collapse of past societies. Which of these factors do you feel are most likely to threaten civilizations today?

- The destruction of forests and other habitats
- Soil erosion and loss of soil fertility
- Water supply and management problems
- Overhunting
- Overfishing
- Damage to native plant and animal species caused by the introduction of new species
- Human overpopulation
- An increase in the impact on the environment of each individual

MORE WORDS YOU'LL NEED

archaeology: the study of ancient civilizations by examining the remains of buildings and objects; also spelled *archeology*

bureaucrat: an official who works for a complex organization or government, especially one who follows the rules too strictly

clan: a tribe or large social group organized according to kinship, or family relations

desecrate: to damage something that is holy such as a religious shrine

excavation: a place where people dig to search for archaeological evidence

sediment: solid material that settles at the bottom of liquids, such as rivers

READ

In this article from a science magazine, biologist and geographer Jared Diamond gives background on the culture, history, and mystery of Easter Island.

Easter's End

Among the mysteries of human history, the mystery of Easter Island (called Rapa Nui in the local Polynesian language) remains unsurpassed. The mystery stems especially from
5 the island's gigantic stone statues (called *moai*), its impoverished landscape, and the extreme isolation of a people living in what might have been an island paradise.

Easter Island, with an area of only 64 square
10 miles[1], lies in the Pacific Ocean more than 2,000 miles west of the nearest continent (South America), and 1,400 miles from the nearest habitable island. Its subtropical location gives it a rather mild climate, while its

---

[1] See Unit 1, page 3, for metric equivalents to measurements used in this article.

volcanic origins make its soil rich and fertile. In theory, these blessings should have made Easter a miniature paradise, remote from problems that beset the rest of the world.

The island **derives** its name from its Easter
day discovery by the Dutch explorer Jacob Roggeveen in 1722. The island Roggeveen saw was not a paradise but a grassland without a single tree or bush over ten feet high. The islanders Roggeveen encountered had no real firewood to warm themselves during Easter's cool, wet, windy winters. Their native animals included nothing larger than insects. For domestic animals, they had only chickens.

Despite the Polynesians' fame as seafaring
people, the Easter Islanders came out to Roggeveen's ship by swimming or paddling canoes that Roggeveen described as bad and frail. The leaky canoes, only ten feet long, held at most two people, and only three or four canoes were observed on the entire island. The islanders Roggeveen met were totally isolated, unaware that other people existed.

Easter Island's most famous feature is its huge stone statues, more than 200 of which
once stood on massive stone platforms lining the coast. At least 700 more, in all stages of completion, were abandoned in quarries or on ancient roads between the quarries and the coast. Most of the erected statues were carved in
a single quarry[2] containing a soft, volcanic stone and **transported** as far as six miles—despite heights as great as 33 feet and weights up to 82 tons. The abandoned statues, meanwhile, were as much as 65 feet tall and weighed up to 270
tons. The stone platforms were equally gigantic: up to 500 feet long and 10 feet high, with facing slabs[3] weighing up to 10 tons.

Roggeveen himself quickly recognized the problem the statues posed. Without wheels
and with no source of power except their own

muscles, how did the islanders transport the giant statues? To deepen the mystery, by 1864 all of the statues standing had been pulled down, by the islanders themselves. Why then did they
carve them in the first place? And why did they stop? Such an undertaking required complex political organization. What happened to that organization, and how could it have arisen in such a barren landscape?

Evidence comes from three fields: archaeology, pollen analysis, and paleontology. Modern archaeological excavations, radiocarbon dating, and linguistic evidence suggest that human activities began around A.D. 400 to
700. The period of statue construction peaked around A.D. 1200 to 1500, with few if any statues erected thereafter. Archaeologists most often **cite** a population figure of 7,000, but estimates range up to 20,000.

Archaeologists have determined that twenty people, using only stone chisels[4] made from hard stones available on the island, could carve even the largest completed statue within a year. Given enough timber and fiber for rope, a few hundred
people could load a statue onto wooden sleds[5], drag it over lubricated wooden tracks or rollers, and use logs as levers to stand them up. Hauling one statue would require hundreds of yards of rope made from plant fibers. Did Easter at one
time have the necessary trees?

---

[2] *quarry*: an open pit or mine from which large rocks are cut
[3] *slab*: a thick, flat piece of stone, wood, or other hard material
[4] *chisel*: a sharp tool for shaping wood or stone
[5] *sled*: a flat vehicle without wheels, used to transport things by dragging or sliding them

That question can be answered by analyzing and dating the pollen[6] trapped in the layers of sediment in swamps and ponds. Pollen analysis shows that during the early years of Polynesian settlement, Easter was not a wasteland at all. Instead, a subtropical forest of woody bushes and trees, including the rope-yielding *hauhau* tree, towered over a ground layer of shrubs, herbs, ferns, and grasses. The most common tree was the Easter Island palm, a relative of the Chilean palm, which grows up to 82 feet tall and 6 feet in diameter. This tall palm would have been ideal for transporting and erecting statues and constructing large canoes.

Excavations of garbage heaps yield an equally surprising picture of Easter's original animal world. Nearly one-third of all bones came from porpoises. Porpoises generally live far out at sea, so they must have been hunted offshore, in big seaworthy canoes built from palm trees. In addition to porpoise meat, the early Polynesian settlers **supplemented** their diet with seabirds, land birds, and rats.

This evidence lets us imagine that Easter's first colonists canoed into a unspoiled paradise and had the resources to develop a complex society. What happened to it? The pollen grains and the bones yield a grim answer.

Pollen records show that destruction of Easter's forests was well under way by the year A.D. 800, just a few centuries after the start of human settlement. Not long after 1400, the palm finally became extinct, not only as a result of being chopped down to clear land for agriculture and provide wood but also because the growing population of rats devoured the nuts necessary for regeneration. The hauhau tree did not become extinct in Polynesian times, but its numbers declined drastically until there weren't enough left to make ropes from.

The **widespread** destruction of the island's animals was just as extreme. Every species of native land bird became extinct and more than half of the seabird species breeding on the island were wiped out. With no trees for constructing big canoes, porpoise bones disappeared abruptly from garbage heaps around 1500. In place of these meat supplies, the islanders intensified their production of chickens and also turned to the largest remaining meat source available: humans, whose bones became common in late Easter Island garbage heaps.

With fewer food sources, Easter Island could no longer feed the chiefs, bureaucrats, and priests who had kept a complex society running. Surviving islanders described to early European visitors how local chaos replaced centralized government and a warrior class took over. By around 1700, the population began to crash toward between one-quarter and one-tenth of its former number. Around 1770 rival clans started to topple each other's statues, breaking the heads off. By 1864 the last statue had been thrown down and desecrated.

As we try to imagine the decline of Easter's civilization, we ask ourselves, Why didn't they realize what they were doing, and stop before it was too late?

The disaster may have happened gradually. Consider the hundreds of abandoned statues. Perhaps war interrupted the moving teams or the last rope snapped. When the last palm tree was cut, palms had probably long since **ceased** to be of economic significance. That left only smaller and smaller palm saplings to clear each year. No one would have noticed the felling of the last small palm.

By now the meaning of Easter Island for us should be chillingly obvious. Today, again, a rising population confronts shrinking resources. It would be easy to close our eyes or to give up in despair. But there is one crucial difference. The Easter Islanders had no books and no histories of other doomed societies. Unlike the Easter Islanders, we have histories of the past— information that can save us. Our main hope is that we may now choose to learn from the fates of societies like Easter's.

---

[6] *pollen*: a powdery material from flowers involved in plant reproduction

READING COMPREHENSION

A. Mark each sentence as _T_ (true) or _F_ (false) according to the information in Reading 1. Use the dictionary to help you understand new words.

.... **1.** The author Jared Diamond blames human behavior for the destruction of Easter Island's ecosystem.

.... **2.** Diamond believes that the culture that originally inhabited Easter Island left once deforestation was complete.

.... **3.** Diamond believes that the statues could not have been built unless the islanders had very sophisticated and modern tools.

.... **4.** The excavation of garbage heaps suggests that the islanders became more desperate in their search for food.

.... **5.** Jared Diamond feels that modern cultures, due to greater knowledge of history and science, are immune to the kinds of ecological disasters suffered on Easter Island.

B. Scan the reading to find the sentences paraphrased below. In the blank, write the first few words of the original sentence.

1. Given these advantages, we might expect Easter Island to be a tiny utopia, a society free from the difficulties of other civilizations.

    ....

2. The people on the island had no contact with people from other places and did not know that there were other humans in the world.

    ....

3. The difficulty of accounting for the presence of these statues was immediately apparent.

    ....

4. Scientific studies show that when the first settlers arrived, Easter Island was not a barren, empty land.

    ....

5. The land could no longer support the political and religious institutions that the community needed.

    ....

READING STRATEGY: Identifying Multiple Causes

Many controversies involve a dispute over causes. Why did/does something happen? Some events may have a single cause, but often we must look for multiple causes, particularly when analyzing changes in human societies. In academic settings, a test or study question may ask about multiple causes.

To establish that an event or condition is a cause, we need to provide a *rationale*: Why is this condition or event relevant? Why is it a possible factor? To be convincing, we need to show that our reasoning is valid and that our explanation is plausible.

A. Read the paragraph and question. Then, drawing on information in Reading 1, complete the table by providing a rationale that explains why each condition is a possible factor in the construction of the statues.

Jared Diamond argues that the statues on Easter Island were constructed by the ancestors of the people living on the island in 1722. To establish this as a plausible explanation, researchers might ask this question: *What conditions made it possible for Easter Islanders to prosper and construct hundreds of large stone statues at one time in their history?*

Condition	Rationale (Why is this relevant?)
1. Pollen analysis shows that the island once had many trees, including hauhau trees.	*Hauhau trees can provide fiber for rope. Rope was needed to drag the statues from the quarry.*
2. Pollen analysis shows that the most common tree was the large Easter Island palm.	
3. There were hard stones available.	
4. There were quarries with soft stone available.	
5. The weather was mild, the soil fertile, and the ocean provided food.	

B. Practice identifying multiple causes by discussing these questions in a small group.

1. According to Jared Diamond, what factors led to the cessation of statue building on Easter Island?

2. According to Jared Diamond, what factors contributed to the collapse of the population on Easter Island?

VOCABULARY ACTIVITIES

Noun	Verb	Adjective	Adverb
cessation	cease	ceaseless unceasing incessant	ceaselessly unceasingly incessantly
citation	cite	....	....
collapse	collapse	collapsible	....
derivation derivative	derive	derivative	....
supplement supplementation	supplement	supplemental supplementary	....
transportation transport	transport	....	....
....	....	widespread	....

A. Here is more information on the Easter Island statues. Fill in each blank with a target word from the chart that completes the sentence in a grammatical and meaningful way.

When Europeans first saw Easter Island, they marveled at the hundreds of statues, called moai, placed around the island's perimeter. Nearly as remarkable as these statues was the condition of the society that had produced them. It seemed to have (1) .... , and all statue carving had (2) ....

All told, researchers have catalogued nearly 900 statues, either on the island or in collections around the world. Interestingly, less than 20% were (3) .... to ceremonial sites. Nearly 400 are still in the main quarry in various stages of completion. Others lie strewn along the roads.

Who were the people that engaged in such (4) .... carving? How did they find enough workers to sustain such (5) .... activity? The adventurer/anthropologist Thor Heyerdahl believed they came from South America, and one writer imagines them coming from outer space. Today, researchers can (6) .... DNA evidence as proof that the islanders migrated from Polynesia, where similar statues are found.

B. The words in bold have more than one meaning. Read these sentences and circle the meaning that best fits the context.

1. Perhaps different groups of Easter Islanders **derived** satisfaction from having a larger statue than their neighbors.

   a. get sth from a specific source   **b.** originate from sth

2. Many argue that the society had already **collapsed** by the time Jacob Roggeveen arrived.

   a. dropped suddenly in value   **b.** suddenly ceased to function

3. Jared Diamond **cited** environmental degradation as the primary cause for the collapse of Easter Island.

   a. quoted sth   **b.** used sth as evidence

4. The book **transported** me back to a time when this fascinating culture thrived on an isolated island paradise.

   a. shipped to a distant place   **b.** created the feeling of being in a different place

---

The word *derive* has the general meaning of something coming from another thing. It is used in many contexts.

*She **derived** great pleasure from listening to classical music.*

*The notion that Easter Island was once heavily forested **derives** from pollen studies.*

*Asphalt is **derived** from petroleum. It is a petroleum **derivative**.*

*Critics complained that the movie was too **derivative** of Steven Spielberg's work.*

Derive is also used to describe word origins. In this context, the noun form is *derivation*.

*The word cease is **derived** from the Latin word cessare. It is a Latin **derivation**.*

C. Work with a partner to find out what these things are derived from. Go online and do some research, if necessary. Discuss your results in a small group.

1. diamonds   3. plastic   5. cocoa

2. paper   4. silk   6. the word *salary*

D. In a small group, discuss which of these practices you feel will become more widespread in the future and why.

1. multitasking at work

2. using odors to enhance movies and video games

3. making movies that are entirely based on digital effects

4. watching movies on handheld devices

5. using robots to do household chores

6. using swarm bots to hunt for things

BEFORE YOU READ

Read this question. Discuss your answers in a small group.

Jared Diamond claims Easter Island's civilization collapsed because it ignored the environmental crisis it had caused. But societies can fail due to reasons outside their control. Possible external factors include

- sudden natural disasters (volcanoes, earthquakes, tsunamis, fires, floods)
- long-term climate changes that affect farming, hunting, and fishing
- diseases affecting people, livestock, or crops
- foreign invasion

What external factors might have played a part in the collapse of Easter Island's population?

MORE WORDS YOU'LL NEED

artifact: an object produced by humans. Archaeologists look for *artifacts* from past societies.

extrapolate: assume that what is true of one thing will be true of another. We can also *extrapolate* by projecting a trend into the future (see Unit 6).

famine: widespread starvation

infighting: fighting among the members of one group

READ

This article from *New Scientist* magazine discusses the work of several researchers who question the validity of Jared Diamond's conclusions about Easter Island.

A Monumental Collapse?

It is a familiar tale of greed, stupidity, and self-destruction. For hundreds of years the inhabitants of Easter Island competed to build ever more impressive statues, depleting their resources
5 to feed their obsession. Ecological disaster was inevitable. As the island's last tree was felled, the society **collapsed** into warfare, starvation, and cannibalism. Rival clans toppled each other's statues. The workers rose up against their rulers.
10 The vanquished[1] were either enslaved or eaten.

   This version of events on Easter Island has become not only the accepted story, but a dark warning about a possible fate for our entire planet. "The parallels between Easter Island and
15 the whole modern world are chillingly obvious," writes Jared Diamond of the University of California, Los Angeles, in *Collapse*. "Easter's isolation makes it the clearest example of a society that destroyed itself by overexploiting
20 its own resources." But is it true, or are we too eager to think the worst of our species?

   There are problems with almost all aspects of this story, say Terry Hunt of the University of Hawaii and his colleague Carl Lipo of California
25 State University, Long Beach. Take the idea that the population was once much larger than the low estimates made by early visitors. "People say, 'Look at all these statues, there must have been

---

[1] *(the) vanquished*: (people) conquered by another group or totally defeated in battle

armies of people to do this,'" says Lipo. Many
conclude that by Roggeveen's time the society
had already collapsed. "But that is just absolute
speculation," Lipo says.

Population estimates based on the remains
of prehistoric settlements are difficult to
validate. Totals range from a few thousand to
20,000. It is an inexact science because no one
knows how many people lived in each house,
and not all settlements have been well studied.
Besides, recent archaeological analyses suggest
a different conclusion. In 2005, a paper by Hunt
and Lipo and another by Britton Shepardson of
the University of Hawaii gave the first thorough
analyses of Rapa Nui's networks of prehistoric
paths. Hunt and Lipo suggest the paths were
built at different times by different groups of
people. There is no evidence of an "interstate
system," but rather a number of separate roads.
"We suggest this indicates smaller groups
working on their own," says Hunt—perhaps
different kin groups rather than workers
operating under the control of a single authority.

Then there is Hunt and Lipo's recent
re-analysis of the date when Rapa Nui was
colonized. Results of radiocarbon dating of
charcoal from a new excavation push forward
the arrival of the first Polynesian settlers by
some 400 years, from an estimated A.D. 800 to
A.D. 1200. Although there is no evidence to say
how many colonizers there were, it is likely that
numbers were small.

When it comes to claims of massive
deforestation, however, the evidence is
undeniable. Soil analysis suggests an estimated
16 million palms once stood on the island, and
deforestation seems to have begun as soon
as the settlers arrived around 1200, and was
complete by about 1500. Yet the reason the
islanders wiped out their forest is still open to
dispute. Some palms may indeed have been cut
down to assist in moving the statues, though
Hunt points out that they would not have
been ideal for the job since they have very soft

interiors. Other trees were used for firewood,
and land was cleared for agriculture. Still, the
blame for the disappearance of the palms might
not rest entirely with people, say Lipo and Hunt.
They point the finger at rats.

However it happened, was losing the forest
really such a bad thing? Some researchers **deny**
that it was all bad. According to the theory of
self-destruction, the massive deforestation
loosened the topsoil[2], which blew into the
ocean, depleting the ground of nutrients and
causing food shortages. However, ongoing
research suggests that erosion was not the
problem people have assumed.

Thegn Ladefoged of the University of
Auckland in New Zealand is analyzing samples of
soil from locations across the island. In general,
the soils are poor, he reported at the meeting
of the Society for American Archaeology in San
Juan, Puerto Rico, in May 2006. **Nevertheless**,
he adds, there is no clear evidence of extreme soil
degradation across the island. "I think people
have extrapolated from one area which does
show extreme degradation to the whole island. I
just don't see it," says Ladefoged.

What is apparent on the ground is the large
number of rock gardens that cover much of
the island's interior, in which crops such as
taro, yams, and bananas were grown. These
take several forms, from windbreaks made of
large lava boulders to piles of smaller rocks
mixed with earth that would have acted to keep
moisture in the soil. Lipo and Hunt suggest that,
given Easter Island's poor soils and relatively
low rainfall—which struggles to top 1,500
millimeters a year—it actually made sense to get
rid of the forest to make way for these gardens,
and to extend agriculture across a greater range
of soils and levels of rainfall.

The earliest gardens seem to date from
around 1300. Christopher Stevenson of the
Virginia Department of Historic Resources
thinks that they were abandoned from about
1600. This would have coincided with a revolt

---

[2] *topsoil*: the outermost layer of the Earth, the part capable of supporting agriculture

against the ruling class, triggered by food shortages when the timber ran out and people could no longer make rafts for deep-sea fishing or hunt the birds and animals that died out with the palm forests. Norwegian anthropologist Thor Heyerdahl, who studied the island in the 1950s, pinpointed the infighting to about 1680, based on a burn layer in the soil. Diamond also settles on a date of around 1680. "The collapse of Easter society followed swiftly upon the society's reaching its peak of population, monument construction, and environmental impact," he writes.

This all seems to support the accepted story of Easter Island history, but not everyone is convinced. Most of the evidence for starvation and cannibalism comes from oral histories, which are "extremely contradictory and historically unreliable," according to John Flenley at Massey University in Palmerston North, New Zealand. He points out that by the time detailed observations were made in the 19th century, the **culture** was virtually dead. Hunt and Lipo suspect that stories of cannibalism, in particular, could have been fabricated by the missionaries who arrived in 1864.

What about the oral history of starvation and conflict? It is possible this could describe events that occurred not before European contact but afterwards. Between 1722 and 1862, an estimated 50 European ships visited Easter Island. By the 1830s, whalers reported widespread sexual disease on the island, says Benny Peiser of Liverpool John Moores University, UK. Slave raids also began in about 1805, and in 1862 and 1863, Peruvian and Spanish slave boats captured an estimated 1,500 local people. After this, reports of smallpox are rife.[3] When missionaries finally arrived, they found a starving people whose society undeniably had collapsed. By 1872, following further slave raids and transports to Tahiti, only around 100 local people were left on Rapa Nui.

Diamond and others **conceive** of these disasters as the final assault on a society that had already destroyed itself. Peiser, along with Hunt and Lipo, thinks the disease introduced by Europeans is a plausible trigger of the only real collapse of the society. They note also that while Roggeveen's impression in 1722 was of "singular poverty and barrenness," there are contradictory descriptions. Peiser **quotes** an extract from the journal of a member of a French expedition that visited in 1786: "Instead of meeting with men exhausted by famine… I found, on the contrary, a considerable population, with more beauty and grace than I afterwards met with on any other island; and a soil which with very little labor furnished excellent provisions."

Lipo and Hunt do not claim to have all the answers. Instead, they aim to make other researchers think more critically about the history of Easter Island. The story of ecocide[4] may usefully **confirm** our darkest fears about humanity but, as Diamond points out in *Collapse*, for every society that self-destructs there is another that does the right thing. It is far from clear that the Easter Islanders made their situation much worse for themselves, but only more evidence will resolve the issue.

---

[3]*rife*: prevalent, widespread
[4] *ecocide*: a word derived from the word *ecology* and the suffix *-cide*, meaning "kill." It is the act of destroying the environment.

READING COMPREHENSION

A. Mark each sentence as *T*(true) or *F*(false) according to the information in Reading 2. Use the dictionary to help you understand new words.

.... 1. Hunt and Lipo doubt that the statue building would necessitate a large population.

.... 2. Hunt and Lipo do not acknowledge that deforestation occurred on Easter Island.

.... 3. Most researchers, including Diamond, deny that the population of Easter Island declined in the 19th century.

.... 4. Peiser, Hunt, and Lipo delay the collapse of the society to after the late 1700s.

.... 5. The author of this article believes that Hunt and Lipo have raised serious doubts about Jared Diamond's account.

B. Scan both readings in this unit for the answers to these questions. First think about the key word you will scan for. Use any annotations or highlighting you have done to help you. Compare answers with a partner.

1. According to Hunt and Lipo's research when was the earliest settlement of Easter Island?

2. Is this date earlier or later than Diamond's date?

3. When was deforestation complete according to Hunt and Lipo?

4. Would Diamond agree or disagree with this date?

5. When did the slave raids begin?

6. Did the article by Diamond mention the slave raids?

READING STRATEGY: Synthesizing Information from Several Sources

Researching a topic may involve synthesizing information from two or more sources. Synthesizing is particularly challenging when the sources do not agree.

You have now read two articles offering somewhat different versions of the history of Easter Island. One is a story of environmental destruction triggered by a frantic effort to build giant statues; the other is a story of a culture collapsing in the face of European expansion, its population weakened by disease and reduced by slave traders. Which account is correct? Could they both be partially correct?

Disagreement is useful because it forces us to reconsider evidence, identify errors, refine our arguments, and adjust our position. Resolving a dispute demands that we clarify points of disagreement and ultimately come closer to the truth. In the Easter Island mystery, we will most likely have a clearer, more accurate history of the island than we would have had if there had been no dispute.

A. Clarify points of agreement and disagreement in the two readings in this unit by completing the chart. Compare answers with a partner.

	Diamond	Hunt and Lipo	Both
Polynesian colonists began to arrive on Easter Island around the year A.D. 1200.		✓	
Forests were destroyed to support agriculture.			
The destruction of forests played a major role in the population's decline.			
Rats contributed to deforestation.			
The island's population peaked at somewhere between 7,000 and 20,000.			
The statues could have been constructed by smaller tribal groups.			
The island is littered with around 700 statues that were never completed or erected.			
Destructive civil wars broke out on the island that left the culture in a weakened state.			
The most severe decline in the island's population occurred as result of disease and forced migration caused by contact with outside societies of Europe and Latin America.			
The island was functioning smoothly when Europeans first arrived.			

B. Write a paragraph in which you list points of agreement concerning Easter Island's history.

....

....

....

....

....

....

....

....

....

....

Noun	Verb	Adjective	Adverb/Conjunction
concept conception conceptualization	conceive conceptualize	conceptual	conceptually
confirmation	confirm	confirmable	....
culture acculturation	acculturate	cultural	culturally
denial	deny	deniable undeniable	deniably undeniably
....	....	....	nevertheless
quote quotation	quote misquote	quotable	....
validity validation	validate invalidate	valid invalid	validly invalidly

A. The words in bold have more than one meaning. Read these sentences and circle the meaning that best fits the context.

1. When Captain James Cook visited Easter Island in 1774, he wrote, "We could hardly **conceive** how these islanders, wholly unacquainted with any mechanical power, could raise such stupendous figures, and afterwards place the large cylindric stones upon their heads."

   a. form an idea   **b.** grasp or imagine a situation

2. **Denied** any contact with the outside world due to the island's remote location, the islanders were entirely self-sufficient.

   a. not allowed   **b.** refuse to admit sth is true

3. Archaeologists learn about **cultures** of the past by recovering and examining artifacts.

   a. ways of life   **b.** art, music, and literature

4. He recommended getting the **quotation** in writing before agreeing to the deal.

   a. a stated price or value   **b.** the exact words

5. Kirch feels evidence from limited areas is not enough to **confirm** Hunt and Lipo's claim that the site at Anakena was the earliest settlement.

   a. say that something is true   **b.** demonstrate that something is true

6. The permit is **valid** for one year from date of issue, at which time it may be renewed.

   a. logical, reasonable, or true   **b.** legal or official

Collocations Chart

Verb	Adjective	Noun	Prepositional phrase
cite	....	evidence, sources, experts, works	....
grasp, understand	basic, broad, simple, general, fundamental	*concept*	....
confirm	....	findings, dates, suspicions, the existence (of sth)	....
seek, ask for, wait for, require	official, independent, final	*confirmation*	in writing
....	traditional, mainstream, pop/popular, corporate	*culture*	....
deny	....	the existence (of sth), the fact, access, accusation	....
....	*valid, invalid*	claim, complaint, point, question, thesis, argument, passport, license	....
question, deny, doubt, assess, prove, demonstrate	....	(the) *validity* (of)	argument, theory, conclusion, evidence, concept
....	*widespread*	destruction, speculation, agreement, availability	....

B. The chart above shows some common collocations, or word partners, for selected target vocabulary. Refer to the chart and complete these sentences. Compare work with a partner.

1. The researchers doubt the .... of the method he used to determine the population of the island.

2. Lab results .... the team's suspicions that the ruins were older than they appeared.

3. They sought independent .... of the test results.

4. The mayor .... all accusations of misconduct brought against him.

5. Chapter 1 introduces some fundamental .... of archaeology.

6. There was .... speculation that the governor would not run for reelection.

7. The study .... evidence from both archaeological investigations and oral histories.

C. Individually or in pairs, write grammatical and meaningful sentences that include these sequences of words.

1. confirm that / widespread

   The investigation confirmed that storms had caused widespread destruction.

2. validity / claim

3. quote / authorities / confirm

4. incessant effort / validate

5. deny / collapse

6. critics / valid complaints / nevertheless, / concept (two sentences)

7. ceased / transport / culture

WRITING AND DISCUSSION TOPICS

1. After considering the evidence presented in the readings and activities in Unit 10, what do you think happened on Easter Island? What is the most plausible explanation for the rise and fall of the moai-carving culture?

2. Ropes, logs, rocks, and fish oil—these are the only tools and materials that Easter Islanders had available. Nevertheless, they were able to lift heavy moai onto a sea wall that could only be accessed from the inland side. Conceive of a way to transport a 75-ton statue from a quarry to an upright position on top of a sea wall. You have a large supply of ropes, logs, rocks, fish oil, and...people—that's it.

3. Here are other historical mysteries where archaeology has played a part. Research one of the topics and find at least two conflicting ideas about it. In an oral or written report, explain the nature of the mystery and describe the disputes surrounding it. State your theory of what happened and give evidence to support it.

   - Lost Colony of Roanoke Island (United States)
   - Mayan Civilization (Central America)
   - Anasazi Culture (North America)
   - Pitcairn Island (South Pacific)
   - The Norse Colony (Vikings) on Greenland
   - The Viking Voyage to North America
   - Ötzi the Iceman (Italian and Austrian border)
   - Dwaraka, a city under water (India)
   - Mummies of Ürümchi (Western China)
   - Stonehenge (England)
   - Nazca Lines (Peru)
   - Camelot (England)

Inside Reading 4

The Academic Word List
(words targeted in Level 4 are bold)

Word	Sublist	Location	Word	Sublist	Location	Word	Sublist	Location
abandon	8	L1, U7	attain	9	L1, U5	**complex**	**2**	**L4, U2**
abstract	6	L3, U5	**attitude**	**4**	**L4, U6**	**component**	**3**	**L4, U3**
academy	5	L3, U1	attribute	4	L3, U10	**compound**	**5**	**L4, U6**
access	4	L1, U2	author	6	L2, U4	comprehensive	7	L2, U7
accommodate	9	L2, U7	authority	1	L1, U6	**comprise**	**7**	**L4, U9**
accompany	8	L1, U2	automate	8	L3, U6	**compute**	**2**	**L4, U8**
accumulate	8	L2, U4	available	1	L3, U5	**conceive**	**10**	**L4, U10**
accurate	**6**	**L4, U6**	aware	5	L1, U5	concentrate	4	L3, U8
achieve	**2**	**L4, U1**				concept	1	L3, U1
acknowledge	6	L1, U7	behalf	9	L3, U9	conclude	2	L1, U6
acquire	2	L1, U4	**benefit**	**1**	**L4, U2**	**concurrent**	**9**	**L4, U5**
adapt	**7**	**L4, U7**	bias	8	**L4, U8**	conduct	2	L1, U9
adequate	4	L2, U4	**bond**	**6**	**L4, U3**	**confer**	**4**	**L4, U4**
adjacent	10	L2, U3	brief	6	L3, U6	confine	9	L1, U10
adjust	**5**	**L4, U3**	**bulk**	**9**	**L4, U9**	**confirm**	**7**	**L4, U10**
administrate	2	L1, U3				conflict	5	L1, U2
adult	7	L3, U6	capable	6	L1, U8	**conform**	**8**	**L4, U7**
advocate	7	L1, U10	**capacity**	**5**	**L4, U9**	**consent**	**3**	**L4, U7**
affect	2	L2, U6	**category**	**2**	**L4, U5**	consequent	2	L2, U3
aggregate	6	L1, U9	**cease**	**9**	**L4, U10**	considerable	3	L3, U8
aid	7	L2, U7	challenge	5	L3, U8	**consist**	**1**	**L4, U2, U9**
albeit	10	L1, U7	channel	7	L1, U3	**constant**	**3**	**L4, U8**
allocate	6	L2, U6	chapter	2	L3, U7	constitute	1	L1, U4
alter	5	L1, U1	chart	8	L3, U10	constrain	3	L1, U8
alternative	3	L1, U10	chemical	7	L2, U10	construct	2	L3, U1
ambiguous	8	L1, U4	circumstance	3	L2, U10	consult	5	L1, U6
amend	5	L2, U9	**cite**	**6**	**L4, U10**	consume	2	L2, U2
analogy	9	L1, U4	civil	4	L1, U4	contact	5	L2, U10
analyze	1	L2, U3	**clarify**	**8**	**L4, U8**	contemporary	8	L1, U7
annual	4	L1, U9	classic	7	L3, U9	context	1	L1, U4
anticipate	9	L2, U3	clause	5	L2, U8	contract	1	L3, U9
apparent	4	L2, U9	**code**	**4**	**L4, U9**	contradict	8	L2, U2
append	8	L2, U10	coherent	9	L2, U5	contrary	7	L1, U6
appreciate	8	L3, U5	coincide	9	L1, U5	contrast	4	L1, U7
approach	1	L3, U1	**collapse**	**10**	**L4, U10**	contribute	3	L1, U9
appropriate	2	L1, U8	colleague	10	L1, U5	controversy	9	L2, U3
approximate	4	L3, U4	commence	9	L3, U9	convene	3	L1, U4
arbitrary	8	L2, U8	comment	3	L3, U3	converse	9	L2, U8
area	**1**	**L4, U1**	commission	2	L3, U9	convert	7	L2, U2
aspect	2	L3, U4	commit	4	L2, U6	convince	10	L1, U3
assemble	10	L3, U10	**commodity**	**8**	**L4, U6**	cooperate	6	L1, U2
assess	1	L1, U8	communicate	4	L3, U2	coordinate	3	L2, U6
assign	6	L2, U9	community	2	L2, U7	core	3	L2, U5
assist	2	L2, U5	compatible	9	L1, U9	corporate	3	L2, U2
assume	1	L2, U1	compensate	3	L3, U4	correspond	3	L3, U9
assure	9	L3, U4	compile	10	L2, U6	couple	7	L3, U1
attach	6	L3, U7	complement	8	L1, U7	create	1	L2, U1

Word	Sublist	Location	Word	Sublist	Location	Word	Sublist	Location
credit	2	L3, U6	enable	5	L3, U10	foundation	7	L4, U4
criteria	3	L3, U3	encounter	10	L3, U5	framework	3	L1, U1
crucial	8	L3, U10	energy	5	L2, U5	function	1	L3, U1
culture	2	L4, U10	enforce	5	L4, U7	fund	3	L3, U3
currency	8	L3, U9	enhance	6	L3, U1	fundamental	5	L4, U4
cycle	4	L4, U5	enormous	10	L3, U8	furthermore	6	L4, U9
			ensure	3	L2, U5			
data	1	L2, U3	entity	5	L4, U5	gender	6	L2, U8
debate	4	L2, U4	environment	1	L2, U1;	generate	5	L1, U5
decade	7	L1, U7			L3, U8	generation	5	L1, U7
decline	5	L1, U2	equate	2	L2, U2	globe	7	L3, U2
deduce	3	L4, U7	equip	7	L2, U3	goal	4	L3, U3
define	1	L3, U2	equivalent	5	L3, U10	grade	7	L1, U7
definite	7	L3, U4	erode	9	L1, U9	grant	4	L2, U9
demonstrate	3	L1, U5	error	4	L1, U10	guarantee	7	L2, U8
denote	8	L4, U6	establish	1	L1, U6	guideline	8	L3, U3
deny	7	L4, U10	estate	6	L4, U6			
depress	10	L2, U4	estimate	1	L2, U10	hence	4	L3, U5
derive	1	L4, U10	ethic	9	L2, U9	hierarchy	7	L3, U4
design	2	L1, U1	ethnic	4	L2, U1;	highlight	8	L4, U3
despite	4	L3, U2			L3, U3	hypothesis	4	L4, U7
detect	8	L1, U6	evaluate	2	L1, U10			
deviate	8	L2, U8	eventual	8	L4, U3	identical	7	L4, U5
device	9	L2, U3	evident	1	L4, U2	identify	1	L4, U2
devote	9	L3, U9	evolve	5	L2, U7	ideology	7	L4, U6
differentiate	7	L1, U4	exceed	6	L4, U1	ignorance	6	L2, U9
dimension	4	L4, U5	exclude	3	L4, U7	illustrate	3	L4, U9
diminish	9	L4, U4	exhibit	8	L2, U5	image	5	L3, U5
discrete	5	L2, U6	expand	5	L1, U7	immigrate	3	L2, U1
discriminate	6	L1, U10	expert	6	L3, U8	impact	2	L1, U9
displace	8	L2, U7	explicit	6	L1, U3	implement	4	L1, U2
display	6	L3, U5	exploit	8	L1, U5	implicate	4	L4, U7
dispose	7	L4, U6	export	1	L1, U3	implicit	8	L1, U3
distinct	2	L3, U7	expose	5	L3, U5	imply	3	L4, U7
distort	9	L3, U6	external	5	L2, U10	impose	4	L1, U10
distribute	1	L4, U8	extract	7	L3, U2	incentive	6	L1, U10
diverse	6	L2, U8				incidence	6	L3, U10
document	3	L4, U9	facilitate	5	L4, U1	incline	10	L1, U7
domain	6	L2, U8	factor	1	L3, U8	income	1	L1, U3
domestic	4	L1, U3	feature	2	L4, U1	incorporate	6	L4, U4
dominate	3	L1, U5	federal	6	L2, U3	index	6	L1, U4
draft	5	L3, U6	fee	6	L1, U1	indicate	1	L2, U4
drama	8	L3, U5	file	7	L4, U6	individual	1	L1, U1
duration	9	L4, U1	final	2	L4, U3	induce	8	L3, U7
dynamic	7	L1, U5	finance	1	L2, U2	inevitable	8	L2, U8
			finite	7	L1, U9	infer	7	L1, U8
economy	1	L1, U7	flexible	6	L3, U9	infrastructure	8	L4, U6
edit	6	L4, U8	fluctuate	8	L2, U7	inherent	9	L1, U1
element	2	L4, U1	focus	2	L3, U8	inhibit	6	L1, U5
eliminate	7	L2, U9	format	9	L4, U8	initial	3	L3, U7
emerge	4	L2, U1	formula	1	L4, U8	initiate	6	L2, U10
emphasis	3	L2, U9	forthcoming	10	L4, U3	injure	2	L1, U1
empirical	7	L3, U4	found	9	L4, U8	innovate	7	L1, U3

Word	Sublist	Location	Word	Sublist	Location	Word	Sublist	Location
input	6	L3, U6	media	7	L1, U5	passive	9	L2, U8
insert	7	L2, U9	**mediate**	**9**	**L4, U2**	perceive	2	L2, U9
insight	9	L3, U7	medical	5	L1, U2	percent	1	L2, U10
inspect	8	L3, U3	medium	9	L2, U?	period	1	L2, U6
instance	3	L1, U6	mental	5	L2, U6	persist	10	L2, U4
institute	2	L2, U8	**method**	**1**	**L4, U9**	perspective	5	L3, U2
instruct	**6**	**L4, U2**	migrate	6	L3, U2	phase	4	L1, U8
integral	9	L1, U4	military	9	L1, U4	phenomenon	7	L2, U5
integrate	4	L2, U7	minimal	9	L2, U10	**philosophy**	**3**	**L4, U5**
integrity	10	L3, U7	minimize	8	L1, U1	**physical**	**3**	**L4, U4**
intelligence	6	L3, U8	**minimum**	**6**	**L4, U5**	**plus**	**8**	**L4, U5**
intense	8	L1, U2	ministry	6	L1, U2	policy	1	L3, U3
interact	3	L1, U8	minor	3	L3, U7	portion	9	L3, U9
intermediate	9	L2, U7	**mode**	**7**	**L4, U7**	pose	10	L3, U1
internal	4	L3, U7	modify	5	L2, U3	positive	2	L1, U5
interpret	1	L3, U3	monitor	5	L2, U3	**potential**	**2**	**L4, U8**
interval	6	L2, U5	motive	6	L1, U6	practitioner	8	L1, U2
intervene	7	L2, U8	mutual	9	L3, U3	precede	6	L2, U4
intrinsic	**10**	**L4, U4**				precise	5	L3, U10
invest	2	L2, U4	**negate**	**3**	**L4, U2**	predict	4	L2, U1
investigate	**4**	**L4, U8**	network	5	L3, U2	predominant	8	L1, U8
invoke	10	L1, U3	neutral	6	L2, U10	**preliminary**	**9**	**L4, U1**
involve	1	L2, U3	**nevertheless**	**6**	**L4, U10**	presume	6	L2, U2
isolate	7	L3, U4	**nonetheless**	**10**	**L4, U7**	previous	2	L2, U5
issue	**1**	**L4, U2**	**norm**	**9**	**L4, U6**	primary	2	L1, U1
item	2	L3, U10	**normal**	**2**	**L4, U2**	**prime**	**5**	**L4, U4**
			notion	**5**	**L4, U9**	**principal**	**4**	**L4, U5**
job	4	L1, U1	notwithstanding	10	L2, U1	principle	1	L3, U9
journal	2	L2, U6	nuclear	8	L2, U7	prior	4	L3, U6
justify	3	L2, U3				priority	7	L1, U2
			objective	5	L1, U10	**proceed**	**1**	**L4, U9**
label	4	L2, U2	obtain	2	L3, U6	process	1	L1, U9
labor	1	L1, U2	obvious	4	L3, U7	professional	4	L1, U5
layer	3	L3, U4	occupy	4	L1, U9	prohibit	7	L3, U10
lecture	**6**	**L4, U2**	occur	1	L1, U2	**project**	**4**	**L4, U4, U9**
legal	1	L2, U3	odd	10	L1, U8	promote	4	L2, U6
legislate	1	L3, U3	**offset**	**8**	**L4, U8**	proportion	3	L1, U10
levy	10	L2, U9	ongoing	10	L3, U3	prospect	8	L2, U6
liberal	5	L2, U1	**option**	**4**	**L4, U7**	protocol	9	L2, U4
license	5	L3, U9	orient	5	L2, U5	**psychology**	**5**	**L4, U2**
likewise	**10**	**L4, U5**	outcome	3	L3, U4	publication	7	L3, U1
link	3	L1, U8	output	4	L1, U7	publish	3	L1, U3
locate	3	L2, U1	overall	4	L2, U6	purchase	2	L2, U9
logic	5	L1, U6	overlap	9	L1, U7	pursue	5	L3, U8
			overseas	6	L1, U1			
maintain	**2**	**L4, U1**				qualitative	9	L3, U9
major	1	L3, U2	panel	10	L1, U6	**quote**	**7**	**L4, U10**
manipulate	**8**	**L4, U4**	paradigm	7	L2, U6			
manual	9	L3, U10	paragraph	8	L3, U6	radical	8	L3, U4
margin	**5**	**L4, U3**	parallel	4	L3, U9	random	8	L2, U7
mature	9	L1, U8	**parameter**	**4**	**L4, U5**	range	2	L3, U1
maximize	3	L2, U8	participate	2	L1, U8	ratio	5	L1, U8
mechanism	4	L3, U9	partner	3	L3, U1	rational	6	L3, U3

Word	Sublist	Location	Word	Sublist	Location	Word	Sublist	Location
react	3	L2, U6	sole	7	**L4, U1**	transport	6	**L4, U10**
recover	6	L3, U4	somewhat	7	L1, U4	trend	5	**L4, U6**
refine	9	**L4, U4**	source	1	L3, U2	trigger	9	L3, U7
regime	4	L2, U10	specific	1	L1, U6			
region	2	L3, U1	**specify**	3	**L4, U6**	ultimate	7	L1, U9
register	3	L2, U2	sphere	9	L3, U7	**undergo**	10	**L4, U1**
regulate	2	L3, U6	**stable**	5	**L4, U5**	**underlie**	6	**L4, U6**
reinforce	8	L2, U5	**statistic**	4	**L4, U7**	undertake	4	L2, U3
reject	5	L1, U7	status	4	L3, U2	uniform	8	L3, U1
relax	9	L1, U8	straightforward	10	L3, U4	**unify**	9	**L4, U5**
release	7	**L4, U1**	strategy	2	L2, U5	unique	7	L2, U1
relevant	2	**L4, U8**	**stress**	4	**L4, U4**	utilize	6	L3, U8
reluctance	10	L2, U4	structure	1	L2, U1			
rely	3	L3, U2	style	5	L1, U4	**valid**	3	**L4, U10**
remove	3	L3, U2	submit	7	L2, U9	vary	1	L3, U10
require	1	**L4, U2**	**subordinate**	9	**L4, U3**	**vehicle**	8	**L4, U3**
research	1	**L4, U2**	subsequent	4	L1, U1	version	5	L3, U5
reside	2	L1, U2	subsidy	6	L2, U2	via	8	L1, U4
resolve	4	L3, U4	substitute	5	L1, U1	violate	9	L3, U6
resource	2	L3, U8	successor	7	L2, U9	virtual	8	L2, U10
respond	1	**L4, U7**	sufficient	3	L2, U10	visible	7	L3, U5
restore	8	L3, U5	sum	4	L1, U10	**vision**	9	**L4, U3**
restrain	9	L2, U7	summary	4	L2, U10	visual	8	L3, U7
restrict	2	L2, U9	**supplement**	9	**L4, U10**	volume	3	L2, U4
retain	4	**L4, U3**	survey	2	L1, U3	voluntary	7	L1, U10
reveal	6	L3, U8	survive	7	L3, U2			
revenue	5	L2, U2	suspend	9	L1, U10	**welfare**	5	**L4, U1**
reverse	7	L2, U7	sustain	5	L2, U4	**whereas**	5	**L4, U2**
revise	8	L3, U6	symbol	5	L2, U2	whereby	10	L1, U4
revolution	9	L1, U1				**widespread**	8	**L4, U10**
rigid	9	L2, U7	tape	6	L1, U6			
role	1	L1, U5	target	5	L3, U10			
route	9	L2, U5	task	3	L1, U8			
			team	9	L2, U6			
scenario	9	L3, U7	technical	3	L1, U6			
schedule	8	**L4, U9**	technique	3	L2, U1			
scheme	3	**L4, U3**	technology	3	L3, U8			
scope	6	**L4, U8**	temporary	9	L1, U9			
section	1	L2, U5	tense	8	L1, U10			
sector	1	L1, U3	terminate	8	L1, U9			
secure	2	**L4, U6**	text	2	L2, U4			
seek	2	**L4, U3**	theme	8	L2, U2			
select	2	L3, U1	**theory**	1	**L4, U4**			
sequence	3	L3, U5	**thereby**	8	**L4, U3**			
series	4	L3, U5	**thesis**	7	**L4, U7**			
sex	3	L1, U3	topic	7	L3, U3			
shift	3	**L4, U9**	trace	6	L1, U9			
significant	1	L3, U10	tradition	2	L3, U6			
similar	1	L2, U1	**transfer**	2	**L4, U1**			
simulate	7	L3, U1	transform	6	L2, U7			
site	2	L1, U6	transit	5	L3, U5			
so-called	10	L2, U8	**transmit**	7	**L4, U4**			